Along for the Ride:
A Collection of Stories from the Fast and Furious World of Stock Car Racing

Larry Woody

Sports Publishing L.L.C.
www.SportsPublishingLLC.com

© 2003 Larry Woody
All Rights Reserved.
photos courtesy of Larry Woody

Direction of production: Susan M. Moyer
Project manager: Greg Hickman
Development: Lynnette Bogard
Copy editor: Cynthia L. McNew
Dust jacket design: Joseph Brumleve

ISBN: 1-58261-696-5

Printed in the United States.

SPORTS PUBLISHING L.L.C.
www.SportsPublishingLLC.com

Contents

Preface v

Lap I:
    Go Where and do What? 1

Lap II:
    Hiddie, I'm Richard Petty 11

Lap III:
    Ralph Earnhardt's Boy 19

Lap IV:
    The Sorrow he's Seen 29

Lap V:
    Coo Coo and Son 41

Lap VI:
    Flash Gordon, Wonder Boy 51

Lap VII:
    It Ain't Bragging if you do it 61

Lap VIII:
    Aggravation in Small Doses 76

Lap IX:
    The Wrecker Driver 85

Lap X:
    The Taxi Driver 93

Lap XI:
    Off to Daytona with Road Hog 97

Lap XII:
    Bruising Bristol 108

Lap XIII:
    Fast Times at Talladega 116

Lap XIV:
    Dynamite Bob and Other Legends 126

Lap XV:
    Bits and Pieces 139

Lap XVI:
  The Big Wheels 150
Lap XVII:
  Sons of the Intimidator 159
Lap XVIII:
  Buckshot-Spraying Cheaters 164
Lap XIX:
  Women, Wendell and Willie 171
Lap XX:
  Ink-Stained Wretches 182

Preface

For over 33 years I have covered stock car racing for *The Tennessean*, the morning newspaper in Nashville, and during that span I have frequently been asked by fans, "Do you know so-and-so?" "What's so-and-so really like?" "Who are the nicest guys in racing?" "Who's the biggest jerk you ever met?"

And the most-repeated question/comment: "Man, what a job—getting paid to travel all over the country, attend NASCAR races, and hang out around the drivers! What's that like?"

My editor, Lynnette Bogard, and I one day were discussing potential book projects, and she asked if I had any ideas. I began to reflect on the great (and some not-so-great but still memorable) drivers I have known. About the wacky people I've encountered. About the good times I've enjoyed/survived with my fellow sports writers on a rollicking racing beat described, by one carousing crony, as "neon journalism." About the many laughs we've shared and the occasional tears we've shed.

I thought about how many times folks have asked me, "What's it really like?" Lynnette and I decided to tell you.

All the stories you are about to read are true. An occasional name has been changed to protect the guilty.

—Larry Woody

LAP I:

GO WHERE AND DO WHAT?

The first stock car race I ever saw, I covered.

It was springtime in the late 1960s, and I was working the Saturday night shift at *The Nashville Tennessean* sports department, assigned to the copy desk, where my duties consisted of editing stories, writing headlines, fetching coffee for the veterans, answering the phone, and listening to a litany of ribald jokes spun by crusty Old Man Penrod, who chain-smoked Camels and manned the score line. Bud Burns, the copy desk editor, was designing the front sports page when his phone jangled.

"Burns here."

Pause.

"What? When? Aw, shit."

Bud slammed the phone back into the receiver, startling Bill (Ice) Isom, who was drowsing peacefully on the rim of the copy desk.

"That dam' Boog—" Bud was so mad I thought he was going to bite through the smoldering cigar that he always kept clinched in his jaw and that smelled like old burning wet rags.

Boog Rollins was the paper's auto racing writer and had acquired, as they say, a taste for the grape. When Boog was sober, there wasn't a better newspaperman on the planet. The other 90 percent of the time, however, Boog was about as dependable as a hen in a hurricane. Tonight was part of that 90 percent.

"Boog's grandmother just died," Bud growled.

"Again?" said Ice, chuckling and lighting his 20th Lucky of the young but already already eventful evening. "What's that make, four times this year?"

"Five," said Bud, "and it sounded like they're holding her funeral down at Tootsie's."

Tootsie's is a world-famous Nashville beer joint where a lot of country singers hung out in the old days. It has a back-alley entrance that leads to the rear of the historical Ryman Auditorium, original home of the Grand Ole Opry. Legendary country stars like Hank Williams used to have a few snorts at Tootsie's, then make a dash out the back to the Ryman in time to appear on stage and wail their ballads to the country over WSM radio. A lot of the songs tended to be about drinking.

Newspapermen also liked to hang out at Tootsie's. Boog was a regular. He wasn't the only one, of course. Back then—remember, this was the late '60s—most all newspapermen (and women) drank. Must have been something in the newsprint. It was an occupational hazard, like ink stains, broken marriages, and getting your fingers caught in the printing press. Ever wonder why newspaper paydays have historically been on Tuesdays instead of Fridays? If newspapermen got paid on Friday, there would never be a weekend edition. At least if they get paid on Tuesday, the smaller weekday editions have a fighting chance to get published.

But here it was, early Saturday evening, and Boog had just called to inform Bud that he couldn't cover the races at Fairgrounds Speedway, as he had been scheduled to do, due to the untimely demise of his beloved granny. Boog couldn't fool Bud, of course—Bud knew they didn't have a jukebox blaring "Honky Tonk Angel" in the background at a funeral parlor.

"Well, hell," Bud muttered around his cigar. "Boog's drunk, and they've got that big race at the Fairgrounds. Lindley, Allison, Farmer, a bunch of the big boys are running." Butch Lindley, Bobby Allison, and Red Farmer were among the legendary drivers who barnstormed the South in those days, challenging the local leadfoots at the little weekly short tracks. Nashville afforded some of the best competition—tough old veterans like Coo Coo Marlin, Flookie Buford, Fat Boy Ryman, Paddlefoot Wales, and a young hotshot who had moved down from Owensboro, Kentucky, named Darrell Waltrip. It figured to be a helluva race. Of all the nights for the racing writer to decide to bury his grandma at Tootsie's.

"We gotta get somebody out to the track," Bud said, scowling around the office.

Raymond Johnson, our sports editor, was up north somewhere at a horse race or boxing match. John Bibb was down south at some fancy golf tournament. F. M. Williams, the University of Tennessee beat writer, was in Knoxville. Jimmy Davy, who covered Vanderbilt, was clever enough to avoid the office at all costs. Our prep writers, Teets and Buckshot, were busy with their spring sports weekend wrapups. Ice, who covered the Dixie Flyers hockey team (his column was titled "Ice on Hockey") was needed on the desk on Saturdays to help Bud get out the big Sunday section. There were three or four other deskmen who, like Penrod, didn't write. They were strictly copy editors. Bud scowled at me thoughtfully, through a haze of blue stogie smoke. I shuffled some copy paper, trying to look busy.

"Woody," he said. "Get your ass out to the track. I need 18 inches for the first [first edition, which went to press about 10:30]. File a write-through for the city [final edition]."

"Huh?" I said, or something to that effect. I had never been to a racetrack. I had never seen a race, not even on TV, because back then stock car races were never televised. TV didn't even acknowledge the existence of stock car racing; the general public looked down on racing as something that rubes and rednecks used as an excuse to escape their trailer parks and go do some drinking and fighting with their buddies. Much too ruffian a sport for TV.

But the papers—at least the Southern papers—covered racing religiously. I had read Boog's stories and I had a general knowledge of how racing worked: some crazy guys climbed into their cars and chased each other in circles around a track, crashing into one another until only one was left standing. He was declared the winner. Or something along that line.

I had never had the slightest desire to watch a race. I was in college, working part-time on the sports department copy desk and serving as an occasional backup writer for "normal" sports. I could write football and basketball and baseball. I could even write hockey if I had to (the difference between hockey and racing is that the hockey players don't catch fire when they crash into each other). But stock car racing?

"Uh, Bud, I don't know anything about racing," I said.

"Learn," growled Bud.

Bud Burns was a burly former semipro baseball and basketball player and an ex-paratrooper with the 82nd Airborne who had parachuted into France on D-Day. I had the feeling that Bud took few prisoners. When Bud said "Go," you went. I walked over to my desk and picked up a notepad.

"Ask for Carver," Bud said as I headed out the door. "He'll help you." Joe Carver was the track's PR director. I'd met him a few times when he'd dropped off press releases at the sports department. He was always friendly, smiling, joking. I liked Joe. Tonight he would be my mentor. And my savior.

I drove out to the Fairgrounds, about 10 minutes from the paper's downtown location, and Joe met me at the back gate. Bud had called ahead, explained Boog's condition, and told Joe that I was coming. He reminded Joe that I'd never seen a race. He told him to take care of me.

Joe did. I don't recall much about the race; I don't even remember who won. It may have been Waltrip, who was rapidly earning a reputation as the greatest driver ever to come through Nashville, and who would go on to become a major NASCAR star. I do remember that there were a lot of wrecks, and that after it was over the security cops had to break up a fistfight in the infield.

What I recall most distinctly was that it was just about the most exciting thing I'd ever seen.

Joe took me into the pits after the race, introduced me to the winner (Waltrip?) and asked most of the questions.

Joe: "Darrell, Bobby said you deliberately knocked him through the fence and that you are a no-account, dirty driver. What do you have to say about that?"

Darrell: "If Bobby can't stand the heat he oughta quit cryin' and take his overrated butt back to Alabama. When he comes to Nashville, he'd better have his hat strapped on tight, 'cause we ain't racin' go-karts here."

Something of that nature.

At one point the interview was disrupted by someone (Red?) who shoved his way into Victory Circle and tried to punch the winner in the nose. This did not happen at Vanderbilt football games.

I may not have known anything about stock car racing, but I knew a great story when I saw one. Action. Drama. Emotion. Harsh words. Controversy.

Our photographer, J. T. Phillips, a crack racing shutterbug, got some terrific shots of the crashes. Bud played my story (OK, Carver's story) alongside J. T.'s dramatic photos.

I guess you could say that the first racing story I ever wrote, I didn't really write. Joe leaned over my shoulder and essentially dictated the story I typed out. But next morning, the best story in the sports section was a racing story that carried my byline.

That afternoon, Boog wandered into the sports department, rumpled, unshaven, and red-eyed (from all the grieving he had done the previous night, I suppose) and told me I'd done a helluva job and he sure appreciated me filling in for him in his time of need and bereavement.

I was a racing writer.

***

NASCAR has always been famous for its contact racing.

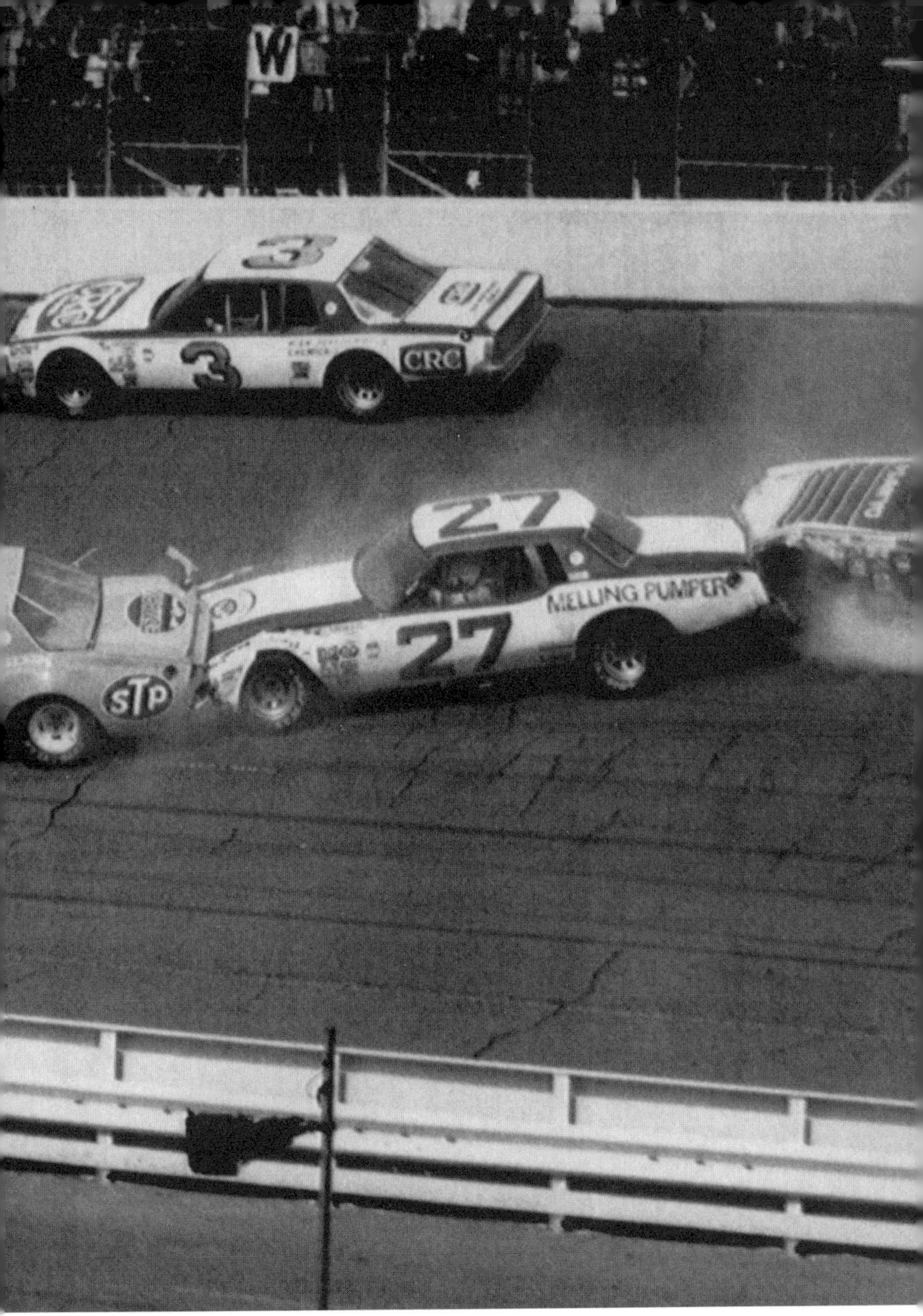
W
3
CRC
27
MELLING PUMPER
STP

Bud Burns liked my racing story. I had made deadline, and as far as Bud was concerned, a perfect newspaper story is one that is set in type and is ready to go when the press starts to roll.

Raymond Johnson, the sports editor, noticed the story when he returned from his trip and checked the back issues before catching the next train to the next big national event. Raymond's only criticism: I should have written more about the fight after the race. Raymond had founded the Golden Gloves, and boxing was his favorite sport.

I gradually came to be considered the unofficial backup racing writer, called on to pinch hit each time Boog's grandmother suddenly passed away. Her passings were becoming more and more frequent, especially on weekends.

I enjoyed covering racing at the Fairgrounds. Joe Carver was super nice and the consummate PR person. If there wasn't a story brewing, Joe would brew one up. The irrepressible Waltrip, who ran his mouth as hard and fast as he ran his race cars, always had something stirred up. When Darrell was around there was never any lack of what newspapers call "good copy."

Bill Donoho, a gruff, pistol-packing former Nashville assistant police chief, was the Fairgrounds Speedway owner, and he took a liking to me. Maybe it was because I was good at cranking out stories—stories that tended to get good play in the papers, and well-played stories translated into good publicity for the track. Donoho, like all race promoters, loved publicity.

I graduated from Belmont University with a major in English, and the U.S. Army promptly grabbed me and shipped me off to Vietnam as a combat rifleman with the 199th Light Infantry Brigade. The Viet Cong didn't seem at all impressed by the fact that I could quote Yeats or recite the prelude to Chaucer's *Canterbury Tales*. I did, however, get to spend a lot of time racing—through the rice paddies with bullets whizzing everywhere. Being in the infantry in Vietnam was almost as wild and exciting as being at Fairgrounds Speedway on a hot Saturday night.

I made it home, entered graduate school, and was trying to decide what I wanted to do with my life when I got a call from

John Bibb (the Bibber, to the staff). Raymond Johnson had retired while I was in the army, and Bibb had been named sports editor. Bibb wanted to know if I'd be interested in returning to work for *The Tennessean*. He said I'd be covering preps, backing up Jimmy Davy and F. M. Williams on Vandy and UT football and basketball, and something else—helping out with racing.

I came back to the sports department. A few months thereafter Bibb summoned me into his office and said he was making me the lead racing writer. Boog, it seemed, had buried one too many grandmothers at Tootsie's.

Bibb explained that I would be covering not merely the Saturday-night fender-benders at the Fairgrounds; he intended to expand the racing beat, and I would travel the country covering big-time NASCAR events.

The sport was growing, Bibb explained, and with that growth came a rapidly expanding fan base, which meant a growing racing readership. Readers were demanding more racing news, Bibb said, and he felt I was the man to deliver it to them. He said he intended to cover NASCAR just like we covered Vandy, UT, golf, baseball, and other "regular" sports.

I had some reservations. I told Bibb I wasn't sure I wanted to get stuck on the "redneck beat," as some fellow staffers referred to the racing assignment. I enjoyed college sports; I'd had my eye on the Vanderbilt beat. Bibb cut a deal: I could still cover other sports (I became the Vandy football and basketball beat writer for 10 years, covered top games throughout the Southeastern Conference for three decades and wrote a twice-weekly column about national sports events), but I also covered NASCAR during that period. I expressed another reservation to the sports editor that day.

"Look, Bibber, I don't know anything about cars and mechanical stuff. I don't know a manifold from a mule's butt. I can barely pump my own gas at a self-service station. How'n hell can I write about Darrell Waltrip's burnt alternator or broken crankshaft?"

"I don't give a damn about Darrell's alternator or crankshaft," Bibb said, "and neither does the average reader. What I *am* interested in—and what the reader wants to know—is what Darrell thinks when he blows a tire at 200 miles per hour and lands on top of Richard Petty. I'd also be interested to know what Richard Petty thinks about it.

"I don't want you to write about cars; this is a sports section, not *Mechanics Digest*. I want you to write about the drivers and all the other wild and crazy people in racing. The people and the personalities. That's what I want to read about. You're the best writer at this newspaper [I suspect Bibb told each of his writers that], and with your wacky sense of humor you have the ability to turn the NASCAR beat into the most creative, interesting, best-read beat in the sports section."

I still wasn't sold.

"Tell you what," Bibb said finally, "just help me out this summer. Cover racing for one season, and if you don't like it I'll find somebody to take over when football starts."

"So I'll just be covering racing temporarily?"

"Yeah," Bibb said. "Just temporarily."

That was 33 years ago.

LAP II:

HIDDIE, I'M RICHARD PETTY

I covered races at the Fairgrounds that summer, not just the weekly Saturday-night slugfests, but the touring regional Sportsman series that made a couple of Nashville stops each season, along with the crème de la crème of stock car racing, the NASCAR Grand National (now Winston Cup) Series.

Up until 1984, NASCAR's top division ran two annual races at Nashville, and during that period I became acquainted with many of the racing giants of that era.

The largest legend of them all was Richard Petty—King Richard—who was at the top of his game at the time.

If NASCAR ran a race and either Petty or David Pearson didn't win, it was an upset. Petty was already a sports icon, a genuine Southern folk hero. He was Davy Crockett on wheels with his trademark cowboy hat, sunglasses, and smile described as "whiter than a catfish's belly" by Birmingham sports writer Clyde Bolton.

A couple of days before covering my first Grand National race, the sports editor told me to go out and interview Petty for a prerace feature. When a legend comes to town you do a story about him. Everybody, even folks who weren't race fans, knew who Richard Petty was. And I was assigned to interview him.

Up till then the most famous driver I'd interviewed in-depth had been Coo Coo Marlin. I drove to the track, feeling like I was heading to Mt. Olympus to have a chat with Zeus. I practiced my introduction:

"Uh, Mr. Petty, I'm a sports writer with the morning paper here in Nashville and if you don't mind, sir, I'd like to ask you about..."

I wandered into the track infield, where teams arriving for the weekend's race were unloading cars and equipment from their haulers. Across the way I spotted Petty's famous red and blue STP Pontiac. ("Pony-ack," as Petty called it.) Beside it was propped a lean figure in sunglasses, jeans, boots, and a cowboy hat. Beneath a droopy moustache he had a black cheroot clamped in his teeth. The King himself. Petty was chatting with a crewman in a greasy T-shirt, who was holding a lug wrench. I walked over and stood, waiting.

The man in the grease-smeared T-shirt noticed me. Petty glanced over his shoulder to see who he was looking at and saw a nervous kid clutching a note pad. I had "Rookie Reporter" branded on my forehead in big, glowing letters.

"Uh, Mr. Petty...?" I began.

"Hiddie, I'm Richard Petty." He stuck out his hand.

I was shaking hands with The King.

I stammered through the introduction I'd rehearsed: "Mr. Petty ... writer ... morning paper ... ask you about ..."

"Why shore, be happy to," Petty said, grinning and pushing back the brim of his cowboy hat with his thumb. "Dad-blamed hot, ain't it? Why don't we git over in the shade while we talk?"

So I sat in the shade with Richard Petty and we talked for about 45 minutes, which is approximately 44 minutes more time than a writer is likely to get with today's average NASCAR superstar who happens to be a mere 199 wins shy of Petty's all-time record of 200.

For many fans, Richard Petty will always be the King.

Petty told me how he enjoyed coming to Nashville, about how he liked the "old-fashioned" night racing on the little half-mile track. He said he and David Pearson were actually "pretty good buddies" despite their fierce rivalry on the track. And "Shoot-far, no," winning never got old no matter how many times he did it.

I was captivated. Sitting there in the shade that afternoon, I became a lifelong Richard Petty fan. I know, I know—the media is supposed to be impartial, objective, and not play favorites. To hell with impartial. Richard Petty is the greatest, most noble figure ever to grace the world of sports as far as I'm concerned.

There, I said it. Call the Columbia School of Journalism and file a complaint.

Petty always won with class and flair and lost with dignity and grace, and he handled stardom with a genuine humility unmatched before or since.

"Never forget where you come from," he said, "'cause some day you may go back there."

In the ensuing years I would interview the titans of sports: Mickey Mantle, Arnold Palmer, Michael Jordan, Terry Bradshaw, Jimmy Connors, Joe Namath. I held court with the venerable Bear Bryant—I can still hear the rumbling voice, smell the Chesterfields and bourbon on his breath.

Wilma Rudolph told me how she overcame childhood polio to win a stack of Olympic track medals.

I got Tom Landry to explain why he wore his hat indoors.

I covered a Muhammad Ali fight in New Orleans, and many years later when I interviewed him, those fists that had flashed with such terrible thunder and power trembled uncontrollably and the great poet/warrior mumbled incoherently.

I once got dog-cussed in public by the seriously disturbed Bob Knight. (I have forgotten the exact question that sent him off ranting and raging and spewing profanities.)

I would cover some 20 Super Bowls, 25 Kentucky Derbies, NCAA Final Fours, major college football bowls, and just about every other major sports event on the continent. No experience,

Along for the Ride 15

David Pearson was Petty's biggest racing rival, but the two were friends off the track.

I believe, made as strong and lasting an impression as the first time I met Richard Petty.

Today, whenever we meet, he always says hello. Actually, he says, "Hiddie there, Woody. How's things in Nash'ful?"

It's been over 30 years since that first meeting, and I still remember the moment: sitting in the sweltering infield at Fairgrounds Speedway, the nervous kid reporter and the legendary racer.

There I sat, sharing a little shade and conversation with The King.

***

All of the times, through all of the years, that I've been around Richard Petty I've never heard him cuss. I did hear him say "cat's ass" once. I don't think that counts.

Petty once considered becoming a partner in Nashville Speedway. He flew in one afternoon, talked with track promoter Bill Donoho for a while, and then departed. Nothing ever came of it. They couldn't come to terms.

"I thought 'Richard Petty Raceway' would have a good ring to it," Donoho told me afterwards.

Nobody in sports has ever had a better relationship with the fans than Petty.

Richard Petty has without question signed more autographs than any sports star or celebrity on earth. He never charged for one. He said it would be insulting to ask for money from someone who thought enough of him to request an autograph.

The King's signature is comprised of gracefully looping swirls and curls. Petty took a class in penmanship to perfect his signing. It isn't an autograph; it's artwork.

***

I interviewed Richard's father, the venerable Lee Petty, one time. It was in a Red Lobster restaurant in Daytona Beach. I walked in and recognized Lee, sitting alone at a booth, eating a bowl of chowder. I walked over, innocently unaware of Lee Petty's reputation among the press as a holy terror, and introduced myself.

He wiped his mouth with his napkin and squinted up at me. Maybe he realized that I didn't realize that I was supposed to be afraid. Maybe he took pity. At any rate, he nodded me into the booth across from him, and for the next half-hour he chatted amicably. I sipped iced tea and took notes. Lee finished his chowder and smoked his pipe and patiently answered every mundane, hackneyed question I dredged up.

"Yes, this place sure has changed," said the man who won the first Daytona 500.

"Naaa, I don't miss racing; I got into it mostly just to make a living." And, "Yeah, I'd have to say that Richard's done a pretty good job."

Next day I mentioned to a veteran writer that I'd had a long conversation with Lee Petty.

"You did what?" he said. "You talked to Lee Petty—and lived to tell about it?"

Over the years I would hear countless horror stories about Lee's cantankerous nature, especially from reporters. Don't dare approach Lee Petty, everybody warned; he's like a grizzly with an abscessed molar. He'll bite your head off. Reclusive. Grumpy. Grouchy. Hates the media.

I don't know about any of that. All I know is that my one experience with him was absolutely delightful.

Today when I think of Lee Petty I think of a gracious old gentleman, sitting at a restaurant booth, contentedly smoking his pipe and seeming to enjoy—or at least tolerate—the company of a kid who had the audacity to intrude on his clam chowder.

***

Lee died in 2000, and later that spring, his great-grandson Adam, 19, was in Nashville to practice for an upcoming race in the NASCAR Busch Series. I asked Adam if I could talk with him for a few minutes.

"Sure," he said, and invited me inside his hauler, where he flopped, teenage-style, into a chair and began to fiddle with a TV remote control.

For the better part of an hour we talked about the immense racing legacy; the Pettys were NASCAR's First Family, their very name synonymous with stock car racing, and young Adam was heir to the throne. Adam discussed the recent passing of his great-grandfather, his special relationship with his grandfather (Adam called Richard "King") and about how determined he was to fulfill his racing destiny.

Adam had grown especially close to his grandfather. His own father, Kyle, was busy with his career and helping oversee Petty Enterprises. Richard, who likewise had been immersed in his racing when Kyle was growing up, had retired as a driver and therefore was able to spend more time with his grandson. The bond between Richard and Adam was special. Everyone could see it. It was as if Richard were recapturing Kyle's lost years through Adam.

As we talked that day, Adam constantly flashed that famous, dazzling, infectious Petty smile. Adam: tall and lanky and smiling, engaging and charismatic. And born to race. Adam had all the Petty genetics. He was made in the King's image. He would continue the reign.

A couple of weeks later he was dead. Adam Petty perished in a crash while practicing for a race at New Hampshire International Speedway.

In a span of a few weeks the Pettys had lost their past (Lee) and their future (Adam). The dynasty was over.

The smile was gone forever.

LAP III:

RALPH EARNHARDT'S BOY

I was working the desk at the sports department one afternoon in the late 1970s when Joe Carver called. Joe was PR director at Nashville Speedway, and there was a big race coming up that weekend. Joe was trying to drum up some publicity.

"I got a driver out here that I think you might be interested in talking to," said Carver.

"Yeah? Who?"

"Dale Earnhardt."

"Who?"

"Dale Earnhardt, from over in North Carolina. Ralph Earnhardt's boy. He's just getting started, kinda rough around the edges, but I think he could be pretty good someday. Maybe not as good as his daddy, but still pretty fair."

I explained to Joe that I was stuck on the copy desk and couldn't come to the track, but if he would bring this Earnhardt guy to the office I'd interview him and see if we could get a story in the paper.

Twenty minutes later Carver strolled in. At his side was a sturdy young man wearing jeans, scuffed boots and an imitation leather jacket. He had a droopy, scraggly moustache and hair down over his ears. Icy blue eyes. Joe introduced us, and instead of shakings hands Earnhardt just nodded and grunted. I noticed that his fingernails were dirty.

Earnhardt slouched in a chair and for the next 10 minutes or so mumbled monotone answers to my questions. At one point I asked him some generic question about the upcoming race.

"Shit if I know," he muttered.

My first impression of Dale Earnhardt: surly redneck.

Over the years my impression of him would change dramatically. I came to like Earnhardt immensely and to admire him greatly. I regarded him as the epitome of the American Dream: a rough-hewn mill-town kid with an eighth-grade education who built a multimillion-dollar racing empire, Dale Earnhardt, Inc., out of sheer grit, will and determination.

I came to realize that Earnhardt was shrewd and intelligent—not book-learned intelligent, but common sense bright. Country smart, they call it. Earnhardt never had a course in mechanical engineering, yet he understood how to make cars go fast, grasping completely the theories and principles behind speed and horsepower. He didn't study physics, yet he understood innately the nuances of aerodynamics. (It was claimed that Earnhardt, a master of drafting on the superspeedways, could "see air.") Earnhardt joked that he graduated from "Winston Cup University."

Earnhardt once addressed the elite Washington Press Club, speaking to an assembly accustomed to presidents and kings, titans of industry, international diplomats, university chancellors and Nobel Prize winners. He totally captivated the audience.

I was not alone in my initial impression of Earnhardt, however. During his formative years in the sport he had a reputation among the media as being gruff, aloof and reclusive. We would later come to realize that he was merely self-conscious. Earnhardt viewed the media as a cadre of college-educated wordsmiths, and when confronted by persons of such lofty academic pedigree he worried about his bad grammar, his lack of formal education, and his absence of social grace.

Gradually he would change his opinion of us—see us as basically just a bunch of good ol' boys hanging out at the track and not above having an occasional brew after work—just as we changed our opinion about him.

I think Dale came to like us. I know we came to like him.

***

Earnhardt enjoyed Nashville, with its country music and honky-tonk hangouts. And Nashville purely loved Dale Earnhardt. An unofficial Earnhardt Fan Club was formed by a young couple named Bill and Carolyn Marlin (no kin to the racing family), and whenever the NASCAR circuit came to town Dale and his team owner Richard Childress got the royal treatment.

I was around Dale a lot in those days. After he grew to trust sports writers he enjoyed having a beer with us and taking racing. And hunting. And fishing. And women. He was still, as Carver put it, a little rough around the edges, but it was apparent even back then that Dale Earnhardt was on a path to a special destiny in the sport.

On the track he was pure hell on wheels. The term "finesse" had been ripped from his dictionary. Earnhardt smashed his way through the field with a rugged, reckless style that left his dented rivals seething in their scrap metal. The fans were, of course, captivated.

Earnhardt's rough and rowdy style quickly earned him the nickname "The Intimidator." Frank Vehorn made that the title of his book about Earnhardt, and it stuck. It was appropriate.

"This ain't tennis," Earnhardt once growled when asked about complaints by fellow drivers that his racing tactics were too rough.

Darrell Waltrip had another name for The Intimidator: "Ironhead." After one run-in with Earnhardt, a furious Waltrip remarked that NASCAR "ought to give bonus points to anybody who takes Earnhardt out."

Waltrip, during a heated battle for the points title, declared: "Earnhardt's not smart enough to win a championship."

But he did. Seven of them. And in the process Earnhardt became widely regarded as the greatest stock car racer in history.

***

In the early years Earnhardt was as wild and reckless off the track as he was on it. I was on the road one race weekend and came stumbling into the motel in the wee, gray hours. As I weaved down the dimly lit hallway toward my room, I met Earnhardt weaving the other way. He was clutching a half-empty Jack Daniels bottle. I got the notion the other half had not simply evaporated over the course of the evening.

"'Lo, Dale," I said.

"'Lo, Woody," said Earnhardt.

Two badly listing ships, passing in the night.

Earnhardt liked to talk about deer hunting. He knew I hunted deer, too, and during one autumn visit to Nashville he asked me if I'd got a deer yet. I told him yep, I'd got two.

"Either of 'em have horns?" he asked with a grin. "I got me nice 10-point buck."

"Yeah, Dale," I said. "I saw you hunting on that fancy stocked game preserve [he had recently been featured on a television hunting show]. I couldn't tell for sure—exactly how close were you standing to that 10-pointer's cage when you shot him?"

Earnhardt whooped with laughter.

***

The big change in Earnhardt came with his marriage to Teresa. Her sense of proper upbringing and refinement seemed to rub off on Dale. Close acquaintances remarked on it, on how Teresa had managed to tame The Intimidator. I don't know that Teresa ever completely domesticated Earnhardt, but at least she housebroke him. He settled down and became a Family Man.

Teresa may have taken away Dale's growl when he was removed from the track, but there was no reining him in when he climbed into his race car. When he flipped on the ignition and his ebony Chevy began its throaty growl, he was the Earnhardt of old: ornery, combative and ready to rumble.

Earnhardt raced the way his daddy had raced a generation before: flat out, no backing off, no apologies. He gave no quarter and asked none.

Earnhardt could, indeed, be intimidating, menacing. Wide linebacker shoulders. Bristling moustache. Steely blue eyes that iced over when he was angry. I believe it was Ed Hinton who wrote the best description of Earnhardt's gaze I've ever read. He said he Earnhardt had the eyes of a Confederate sharpshooter hunkering on a ridge, coldly squinting down the barrel of his rife as he picked off Yankees.

Earnhardt had a wicked sense of humor. A steakhouse in the Carolinas once named a huge, thick, choice sirloin "The Intimidator" in his honor. When Dale heard about it he suggested they ought to name another entree after one of his racetrack rivals, the diminutive Geoff Bodine, with whom Earnhardt had recently clashed.

The Geoff Bodine special? "Chicken and Shrimp," sneered Earnhardt.

Rusty Wallace once complained about Earnhardt's rough racing. When word got back to Earnhardt, he exploded.

"Any time that son of a bitch wants to go toe to toe with me, he knows where I'm at," he snarled.

Earnhardt also threatened to give Darrell Waltrip "a good ass-whipping" one day when Waltrip had been dogging "ol' Ironhead" about something or other.

"If Waltrip knows what's good for him he'd better button that goddamn big mouth of his," Earnhardt warned, "or I'll button it for him!"

Earnhardt and Waltrip eventually became close friends; Earnhardt provided Darrell with a car to drive during one difficult period in the twilight of Waltrip's career. Stevie, Darrell's wife, made a practice of handing Earnhardt a slip of paper on which she had written a message of Bible scripture before each race. Earnhardt had one of Stevie's scriptures in his car the day he crashed and died.

***

Earnhardt relished his rough, ornery image. It wasn't fake; he really was rough and rugged and not above giving someone "a good ass-whipping" if he thought they deserved it.

A report circulated that Earnhardt once caught a poacher on his farm who had illegally killed a deer out of season. Earnhardt pummeled the unlucky poacher to within an inch of his life.

But there was also another side to Earnhardt that the public and his legions of fans seldom if ever saw and didn't know existed. I got a rare glimpse of it once, by accident.

It was the weekend of a race at Bristol. Track officials had arranged for several of the top drivers to make a public appearance at a nearby convention center. The place was jam-packed by excited race fans, anxious to get an up-close look at their heroes. The format called for the drivers to sit on stools on the stage, facing the audience while a master of ceremonies passed a microphone around and the drivers took questions from the crowd.

The event was supposed to start at seven p.m. All the drivers were on hand, ready and waiting, in a room behind the stage. I had decided to attend the event and write a story about what sort of zany questions fans asked their favorite drivers—and what sort of wacky answers the drivers gave in response.

The MC leaned into the room and said it was time to start. The drivers filed out and took their places on stage. One seat was vacant, however. Earnhardt's

I glanced back down the hallway and there was Earnhardt, squatting down beside a wizened old woman in a wheelchair. Her wispy gray hair was drawn back in a bun, and she had a shawl over her legs. In one frail hand she grasped a cheap felt pennant bearing Earnhardt's famous No. 3. Her other hand was being held by Earnhardt, as he knelt on the floor, softly talking to her.

The nervous MC poked his head around the corner. "Uh, Dale, we're ready to start now."

Earnhardt didn't look up. He continued to talk with the old woman. I couldn't hear what he said, but a smile broke over her wrinkled, weathered face. Earnhardt grinned.

After a couple more minutes, Earnhardt got to his feet, leaned over, and kissed the old woman on the forehead. He patted her on the hand, and then walked toward the entrance to the stage, where the audience was waiting for the evening's main attraction.

The old woman's eyes sparkled; from tears, I think.

As he passed me in the narrow hallway, Earnhardt winked at me. "'Lo, Woody," he said.

"'Lo, Dale."

It was a deeply moving scene, a captivating, revealing moment. Think about it: there were no cameras present, no TV, no PR flaks, as Earnhardt knelt beside the old woman. He wasn't doing it for show; he didn't even know he was being observed. He did it simply because he wanted to, because for some reason he was touched by the old woman and cared enough to pause a few minutes and bring a little light into her life.

Often now, when my thoughts stray to Dale Earnhardt, it is not the wild and reckless racer I see, not the macho daredevil, grinding his way through the competition. It is not a scowling, flinty-eyed visage that comes to mind.

No, what I see is Earnhardt, kneeling beside an old woman in a wheelchair, holding her hand and talking softly to her.

Corny? Maybe. But genuine. That's my most enduring impression of The Intimidator.

***

I was at Daytona on Feb. 17, 2001, the day Dale Earnhardt died. Like millions of others watching at the track or around the country on TV, I saw his car spin and crash into the fourth-turn wall on the final lap of the Daytona 500. Like most others, I didn't think it looked that bad at first. I figured Earnhardt might be banged up a little, and that he probably would limp into Victory Circle in a few minutes and join in the celebration being held for his driver, Michael Waltirp, who was savoring his first career win.

I was well into my story about Waltrip's stirring, long-awaited triumph when Gary Long of the *Miami Herald*, sitting beside me in the press box, leaned over and whispered urgently, "Hey, I just heard on the radio that Earnhardt may be hurt pretty bad."

I stopped typing. If Earnhardt was badly injured, that would need to go high in the story, possibly even in the lead. After all, Dale Earnhardt was by far the most celebrated driver in NASCAR; everyone else, even Jeff Gordon, raced in his shadow.

I watched Gary as he continued to monitor his radio. Suddenly his face turned ashen. That's not just a figure of speech; his face literally paled. He turned to me, stunned.

"Dale's dead," he said.

"Naaaa ..." I began. There had to be some mistake.

"That's what somebody just reported from the infield care center," Gary said, adding softly, "Good God. Dale Earnhardt's dead."

Gary reached for his phone and began urgently pushing buttons, calling his paper.

"Guys," he said into the receiver, "Earnhardt's just been killed here at Daytona."

Pause.

"No, it's no joke. That's what being reported. I'll get back to you when I learn something more."

Word by now had begun to filter through the press box as other writers monitored the radio transmissions. What had been a busy clatter of word processors and squawky tape-recorded replays of Waltrip's victory speech gradually fell silent.

Suddenly the voice of NASCAR president Mike Helton came over the PA system.

"This is the hardest announcement I've ever had to make," Helton said somberly. "We've lost Dale Earnhardt."

There were gasps, followed by an occasional muffled sob, throughout the press box.

I immediately called my office. The news had not yet broken over television. I told my editor that Earnhardt was dead. Killed on the last lap of the race about 20 minutes ago.

Silence. Then, softly,

"God-a-mighty."

***

The nation, at least the South and Southeast, has seldom if ever mourned a death the way it mourned Dale Earnhardt's. Not Bear Bryant's. Not even Elvis's. Kennedy's, perhaps, but I was too young to remember.

In Nashville alone, six separate memorial services were held for Earnhardt. On a radio show I do, fans would call in to discuss Earnhardt's death and break down in sobs.

I was assigned to cover Earnhardt's memorial service the following Thursday in Charlotte. (Rumor had it that the burial had been held the day before at a private location, attended only by members of the immediate family.)

I drove to Charlotte on Wednesday night and rose early Thursday morning. A sleety rain was falling. I went to the church, where an entire parking lot was filled with TV satellite trucks. Only a few members of the media had been told they could attend the service. All roads into the church were blocked off, manned by security officers.

I went in and took a seat in the back. An organ played softly as the church gradually filled: Earnhardt's family and relatives, almost every NASCAR driver and his family, crewmen, team officials and NASCAR executives.

Earnhardt's family minister spoke briefly. He was followed by a NASCAR chaplain. Randy Owen sang. At the conclusion, Teresa Earnhardt, dressed in black and appearing frail, stepped to the podium and whispered, "Thank you. Thank you." And it was over. The crowd slowly began to file from the church.

Outside, I encountered Junior Johnson, the legendary racer whom author Tom Wolfe immortalized as *The Last American Hero*. Standing in the cold drizzle, I asked Junior what he thought about Dale Earnhardt.

"He was the best race driver there ever was," Junior said. "Ain't never been one like him before, and I doubt that there'll ever be one like him again."

***

After the service I drove on to Rockingham, N.C., site of the next race. As I wound along the state highway that slices through the countryside, I began to notice the signs. They were in yards, in store windows, even on church marquees.

"Goodbye, Dale."

"God Bless Dale Earnhardt."

"Farewell to The Intimidator."

And often, just a simple black No. 3.

Everybody, is seems, is familiar with that black No. 3. Last spring some friends and I were in the remote Canadian village of Red Lake, in Northern Ontario, on a fishing trip. On the morning before we were to catch a bush plane on up to the lake we were going to fish, I was walking down the street when I noticed a rust-chewed old pickup truck sitting by the curb.

On the back window was pasted a black No. 3. Even in the wilds of Canada, The Intimidator had his fans.

Later I mentioned to one of my fishing buddies my amazement at spotting Earnhardt's No. 3 way off up there.

"Old Earnhardt," he mused. "He was a helluva race driver, wasn't he? Did you know him very well?"

Yes, I said. I knew Dale Earnhardt pretty well. I met him a long time ago.

LAP IV:

THE SORROW HE'S SEEN

It was Friday afternoon, the day before the big Grand National (now Winston Cup) race at Nashville Speedway, and I was chatting with Bobby Allison in the track infield when a local TV crew strutted over.

A bit of perspective: Back in those days—the early1970s—TV treated NASCAR racing as the proverbial red-headed stepchild of sports. The Daytona 500 would get a brief mention, usually toward the end of the sportscast, and if a recognizable driver was killed in a race, his death might warrant a blurb, along with the graphic footage.

That was the case with Nashville TV stations, except twice a year when the Big Show rolled into town. Then the local stations would grudgingly allow racing a few minutes of precious airtime. They would send a crew out to the track to scrounge up some sound bites from some of the top drivers, and maybe capture a crash or two on film.

This was one of those times, and Allison was one of those top drivers, a charter member of the famed Alabama Gang and one of the sport's most recognized racers.

When the great TV god consented to grace a race with its presence, drivers were expected to drop whatever they were doing and heed its beck and call. After all, they were being given a rare honor, not lightly bestowed, to BE ON TELEVISION.

It was not at all unusual, back then, for a TV crew to simply barge up and interrupt a driver no matter what he was doing—working on his car, deep in conversation with his crew, talking with fans—and say,—"Hey, pal, we need you over here a minute!"

Usually the driver would immediately tear himself away from whatever he was doing and meekly obey the command of the great TV god. That's what happened that afternoon at Nashville Speedway—up to a point.

Bobby and I were in the midst of a conversation when a TV reporter, cameraman in tow, interrupted us.

"Hey, Bobby! Listen, I need you to—"

He didn't get to finish.

"I'll be with you in a minute, fellows," Allison said, not entirely pleasantly. "Right now I'm talking with Larry Woody. I'll get with you when we're finished."

The TV guy was so shocked he almost dropped his hair spray. I've been a Bobby Allison fan ever since.

***

I suppose it's because I think so highly of Allison that I've agonized so terribly about him over the years as I have followed his travails and tribulations. Nobody in the history of sports has endured more pain and suffering, more heartbreak and despair, more trials of the body and spirit, than Bobby Allison.

Just to observe it has been heart-wrenching; to have actually lived through it, as Bobby has? Unthinkable.

I have often wondered: what has he done to deserve this? The answer keeps coming back: nothing. Absolutely nothing.

Allison is a good, decent man. He is honest and honorable, a man of strong personal values and deep religious convictions. Yet what should have been his golden years, a time to bask in the twilight of a brilliant career, has been sheer torture.

I was not at Pocono Raceway that fateful afternoon in 1988 when Allison crashed, but I've seen the photos and I can't believe he lived through it. The doctors couldn't believe it, either. Allison's body was broken and torn, his skull fractured, his brain injured. Even after a year of painful physical rehabilitation he was far from recovered.

Allison held his first press conference almost year after his injury at a Birmingham rehab center, and I drove down to attend. When Allison shuffled out to meet the media, leaning on a cane, I didn't recognize him. He was stooped and drawn. His speech was halting and fragmented. His face twisted and contorted as he struggled to form a thought, then verbalize it.

It was painful to watch. It wasn't just Allison's robust health that had been stolen; he also had been robbed of much of his memory. He had won the Daytona 500 earlier in the season, followed across the finish line by his son Davey. It was perhaps the proudest moment of his career—and he couldn't remember any of it.

"I know I won Daytona and I know Davey was second, because I've seen the tapes," Bobby said. "But for the life of me, I can't recall a thing about that race. It's all a blank."

One of the greatest careers in NASCAR was over. But as agonizing as that realization was for Allison, whose entire life had been dedicated to racing, the worst was yet to come.

One of his sons, Clifford, died in a crash at Michigan Speedway. A year later his other son, Davey, was involved in a fatal helicopter crash at Talladega. I had been at Talladega the day of Davey's crash. Jim Freeman, PR director at Talladega Superspeedway, had called several members of the media earlier in the week and invited us down to cover a practice session by David Bonnett. In truth, we were there to meet David's father, Neil, who was planning a comeback after a serious crash.

We ate lunch in the infield media center, interviewed David and Neil, and then I headed back to Nashville to write my story at the office.

A young Bobby Allison during his early racing days.

When I walked into the sports department some four hours later, the editor said, "Any word yet on Davey?"

I didn't know what he was talking about. He said the Associated Press was reporting that Davey Allison had crashed his helicopter at Talladega that afternoon and had been critically injured. Family friend Red Farmer was a passenger and had also been injured. Neil Bonnett had dragged Davey and Red from the whirring wreckage.

I called Freeman. He said the crash occurred about 30 minutes after I left the track. Davey was attempting to set his helicopter down in the infield when it flipped over. Freeman said it didn't look good for Davey.

Davey Allison died that night, and with him died a little bit more of Bobby Allison. Two bright young sons. Two wonderful young men, entering the prime of their lives. Both bursting with promise and potential. Both gone in a heartbeat.

A few years later I was talking with Bobby and I asked him how he managed to cope with such terrible loss, such devastating heartbreak.

He looked at me with sad eyes and said, "You go on. What's the alternative?"

Allison continued. "You get up each morning and try to get through that day. You go to bed that evening and try to get through the night. You get up the next morning and start all over—just trying to make it through one day at a time. That's all you can do. You can't just go off and sit down and give up."

The cruel fates still weren't through with Allison. He tried to keep a racing team afloat, but it floundered and he lost everything.

"I made the mistake of trusting some people who, as it turned out, weren't very trustworthy," he explained.

Allison's personal torment continued. The anguish and pain that Bobby and his wife Judy were forced to endure put such a strain on their 30-year marriage that it gradually unraveled. You could say that it broke under the sheer weight of their grief. They separated.

Allison had lost it all: his health, his racing, his sons, his livelihood, and his marriage.

Yet, somehow, he persevered. He showed up at races. He talked openly about his travails. He never wallowed in self-pity. Bobby Allison is an oak tree.

In recent years things have gotten better—clearly having no other way to go.

Bobby and Judy reconciled and reunited. Some friends gave Bobby jobs as a consultant. Everywhere he goes he is paid deserved tribute as one of NASCAR's all-time greats. His health continues to improve, although some memories remain washed away forever. (Cruelly, only the good memories; the bad ones remain fresh and haunting.)

He goes on. One day at a time.

***

I never knew Clifford Allison that well, but I became fairly well acquainted with Davey. Lean and handsome, bright-eyed and energetic, with streaks of youthful mischief. And blessed with his father's incredible racing talent.

At the time of his death, Davey had developed into one of the bright young stars in NASCAR's galaxy. He was on course to become a major superstar in the sport. In over 33 years of covering racing I have asked one driver for an autograph: Davey Allison. I don't think the media, as a rule, should take advantage of its access to drivers to pester them for autographs, but I violated my rule one time for a young relative in North Carolina. She was a devout Davey Allison fan and she pleaded with me to get his signature for her.

I was strolling through the garage one day at Darlington when I noticed Davey sitting alone beside his transporter. On the spur of the moment I walked over, said hello, and told Davey about my relative, one of his biggest fans. I had my reporter's notebook in my pocket. I told Davey that if he would scribble his name on a page, I'd tear it out and mail it to her.

"What's her name?" Davey asked. I told him it was Mary Ann. "Just a minute," he said, and disappeared inside his hauler. He reappeared moments later holding an 8x10 PR photo of himself. He sat down and signed it, "To Mary Ann with best wishes. Davey Allison."

He was, indeed, his father's son.

***

Davey's widow, Liz, moved with their children Robbie and Krista from their home in Hueytown, Alabama, to Nashville not long after Davey's death. Liz explained why. "I'd be walking down the street with the kids and people—complete strangers—would stop me and start telling me how much they loved Davey and how terribly they missed him... and then they would just break down and start crying.

"While I appreciated their concern and sympathy, after awhile I decided that atmosphere was not good for me and not healthy for the kids. No matter how awful a loss you suffer, you can't live the rest of your life immersed in grief. We needed to get away."

A couple of years ago Robbie, at age eight, talked his mom into buying him a small-sized race car and allowing him to race it at Twin Fountains Speedway, a little just-for-fun track outside Nashville.

Robbie painted his father's famous number 28 on the side of his car and he wore one of his father's old Texaco racing helmets. He looked like a miniature Davey Allison.

I told Robbie I wanted to write a story about him in the newspaper. He handled the interview like a seasoned professional. Like an Allison.

"I'm going to be a race driver when I grow up," Robbie said, proudly posing beside his little race car. "Just like my daddy."

***

Liz was right; you can't live your life immersed in grief and pain and sorrow, and there were some bright spots, moments of hope and humor, entwined with the Allison family's tragedies. Leave it to old pal Neil Bonnett to help bring it out.

Allison recalled one occasion when Bonnett visited him in the hospital. Bobby's speech disorder made it difficult for him to verbalize and articulate his thoughts. Neil at the time was recuperating from a serious crash of his own that had left him suffering bouts of amnesia.

"Between me trying to say what I was thinking and Neil trying to remember what he was talking about, we had a helluva conversation," Bobby chuckled.

***

Bobby Allison was involved in one of the most memorable moments in NASCAR history—a defining moment, as it turned out. It happened one afternoon during the final laps of the 1979 Daytona 500 as Cale Yarborough and Bobby's younger brother Donnie were dicing for the lead.

They sideswiped a couple of times, neither giving an inch of asphalt, then both went spinning off the track. They jolted to a stop in the infield.

Bobby, who had been running on back in the field, immediately pulled off the track, jumped from his car, and ran over to check on Donnie.

Then he made the mistake of "checking" on Cale.

Suddenly a free-for-all erupted. Fists were flying and helmets were swinging and all three drivers ended up brawling in the mud.

"The fight was more excitin' than the race," chortled Richard Petty, who darted past the melee and claimed the victory. "I sure would have liked to have stopped and watched it, but I was in kinda of a hurry right then."

Years later the combatants would joke about the fray.

"I know why Donnie was mad," Yarborough said, "but to this day I don't know why Bobby felt that he had to run over and get into it. He poked his nose in there, and he got it punched."

Speaking of noses: "Aw, I wasn't fighting," Bobby said. "I was just swinging my fist around to get a little exercise and Cale kept putting his nose in front of it."

The brawl provided a dramatic finish to the first NASCAR race ever televised live flag to flag. An ice storm had hit earlier that day, socking most of the nation indoors—in front of their TVs. Suddenly, the nation was captivated by the CBS spectacle of brawling race drivers, swaggering daredevils whose beating and banging on each other was not restricted to the racetrack. Millions of viewers were tuned into NASCAR that day for the first time. They would remain tuned in.

"NASCAR called Cale and Donnie and me in and chewed us out," Bobby recalled years later. "They said we had embarrassed the entire sport on national TV. Then they immediately began using footage of the fight to promote next year's race. That afternoon we gave NASCAR the greatest publicity it's ever had, and they've never even thanked us for it."

***

A few years later another Allison incident would inspire a major NASCAR rule, which today remains one of its most controversial.

Allison was racing at Talladega Superspeedway when his 3,600-pound Buick swerved out of control and went airborne. At the time, cars routinely ran speeds in excess of 200 mph on the mammoth 2.6-mile track. (Bill Elliott had been clocked at a breathtaking 212 mph just prior Allison's airlift.)

Allison's car sailed through the air and up onto the retaining wall. It ripped down several hundred feet of metal fence and almost cleared an eight-foot-high front stretch wall. A few more feet, perhaps inches, and it would have gone tumbling into the packed grandstands where the carnage would have been horrendous. My wife was sitting about 10 rows from the crash site that day.

Cale Yarborough shares a laugh before a race.

NASCAR from that point on required all cars to use speed-sapping restrictor plates when racing at Talladega and Daytona, even though some drivers contend that the plates actually make the racing more dangerous because the faster cars can't break away from the slower ones. They remain bunched in a tight, dangerous clot.

But NASCAR is determined to at least keep the cars on the track and out of the clouds.

Allison, a dedicated pilot, remembers those frantic moments when he went airborne.

"I knew I was in trouble when I went sailing through the air," he deadpanned, "because I hadn't received clearance for takeoff."

***

Allison has a stubborn streak in him. Maybe that's what made him such a great racer. He was too stubborn to lose.

But there is also sadness to his stubbornness. Allison and Darrell Waltrip were archrivals on the track, tough hard-nosed competitors who refused to budge an inch, and their battles were legendary. Waltrip eventually let it go, forgave and forgot, but Allison never has.

Years after his injury-forced retirement, the mere mention of Waltrip's name causes Bobby's mouth to harden and his eyes to grow cold. Some believe it is because Bobby felt, during their racing days, that Darrell had been overly tough on Davey.

Allison, a devote Catholic, once told writer Ed Hinton: "I may burn in hell for it, but I can't bring myself to forgive Darrell Waltrip."

Ironically, Allison and Waltrip will forever be linked in the NASCAR record books. They are tied for third place all-time, each with 84 victories. (Allison still claims he won one race that he didn't get credit for. Stubborn.)

Waltrip ran his final race in 2000, at Atlanta Motor Speedway. Allison was on hand, but not to help celebrate his old rival's "Victory Tour." He said he just came to watch the race.

I bumped into Bobby in the garage the afternoon before race day. I asked him if tomorrow wouldn't be an appropriate time for the two battle-scarred old warriors to finally bury the hatchet. After all the years, the epic battles, the verbal sparring, the hard feelings, they would both finally be retired. Why not shake hands with Waltrip and ride off into the sunset together as friends?

"I guess you're right," Bobby said. "I guess that's what we ought to do." But he never did. Too proud, too stubborn.

***

Eddie Gossage was the PR director for Miller Brewing Company, sponsor of Allison's car during some of his glory years. Gossage is a Nashville native who served a brief stint in the *Tennessean* sports department before getting fired (more on that in a later chapter).

When the tour came to Nashville, Eddie always invited me to dinner with him and Bobby. Allison's favorite resaurant was Uncle Bud's Catfish in Franklin. Bobby purely loved deep-fried catfish. The catfish were always hot, the beer always cold, the stories always fun.

Allison was at the peak of his profession. His health was good, his legacy was secure, and his sons were budding into fine young men and splendid racers in their own right. For Bobby Allison those were good times, the best of times.

If only they could have lasted.

LAP V:

COO COO AND SON

Coo Coo Marlin always had a streak of bulldog in him. He was a stubborn cuss, tough as a truck stop T-bone, and when he sank his teeth into NASCAR Grand National (now Winston Cup) racing back in the 1960s he refused to let go no matter how long and how hard he was kicked and cuffed and pummeled. He just growled his defiance through clenched teeth and bit down harder.

Coo Coo ran in NASCAR's top division for a dozen years and never won a points race—never had much of a chance, really, competing against the "Hot Dogs," as he called his well-financed rivals.

Coo Coo was an "independent" driver who raced without any major corporate backing. He was riding a mule in the Kentucky Derby, but somehow he hung on and hung in all those years. He was one tough old bulldog.

After he turned the keys over to his son Sterling, I asked Coo Coo if he had any regrets as he looked back on his career.

"Naw, not really," he said. "I figure I did the best I could what I had to work with. I turned down a few offers that might have made a difference, but I always liked to be my own boss."

Then he added, "Well, yeah, I guess I do have one regret. Just once I'd have liked to have seen what I could do against the Hot Dogs in equal equipment. I always thought I was as good a driver as they were, but I just didn't have the equipment to keep up with them."

Before Coo Coo moved up to the big leagues, he raced for years at Nashville Speedway. There, on equal footing and on a level playing field, he was virtually unbeatable. He won four track championships and earned a reputation as a driver you didn't trifle with.

Coo Coo was as tough off the track as he was on it.

"We sorta enforced our own rules back then," he explained, a wry grin sneaking across his craggy face.

"We didn't need no fancy rule book. If there was a dispute, hell, we settled it amongst ourselves after the race. Everybody carried a lug wrench, and it wasn't just for changing tires."

Coo Coo didn't acquire his nickname from his driving style (although some of his dented rivals probably thought it would have been appropriate). He was born Clifton Burton Marlin but as a toddler had trouble pronouncing "Clifton," when asked his name. It kept coming out in pieces.

"Coo Coo." It stuck.

Marlin farmed a sizeable spread near Columbia, Tennessee, about 50 miles south of Nashville. Cattle, tobacco, corn, hay. He toiled in the fields all day, tinkered on his race car at night, and spent his Saturdays swapping sheet metal at Nashville Speedway.

It was a tough life, for a tough man.

Sterling inherited his father's toughness and tenacity, his stubbornness and perseverance. Lucky for him he did. He would need it.

Sterling followed his father's trail through the weekly ranks at Nashville Speedway, where he claimed three track championships, one shy of his father's record, and on into Winston Cup. There he started 278 races over 17 years without a win.

Then, finally, one dazzling day in Daytona ...

***

Sterling won the 1994 Daytona 500. His first big-league victory came in NASCAR's biggest race. Two generations of Marlins had raced over a span of four decades, and finally a Winston Cup trophy had the family named engraved on it.

Sterling dedicated his Daytona 500 triumph to his father.

"Daddy raced all those years without a win," Sterling said. "This one's for him."

I covered Sterling's career at the Fairgrounds. He began racing in his late teens, part of what the media dubbed the "Kiddie Corps"—four hot young drivers with lead feet and golden dreams. Mike Alexander, Tony Cunningham, Chubby Crowell and Sterling.

They waged some memorable Saturday night slugfests around the five-eighths-mile oval, and gradually Marlin and Alexander began to separate themselves from the pack. They were both extremely talented, extremely ambitious, and the track literally was not big enough for both of them.

The Marlin-Alexander rivalry became more and more heated. It often spilled over into the stands, where fan loyalty was equally divided. At times fists flew.

"Me and Mike didn't have any problem with each other," Marlin insisted. "We raced hard, but when the race was over, that was it and we got along fine. It was the fans and some of the boys on the teams that stirred up a lot of the trouble. But I guess that was just a part of it."

A brief aside: many racing observers at the time thought that of the two sizzling young racers, Alexander had the edge over Marlin in terms of big-league potential. Alexander was bright and articulate, as smooth off the track as he was on it, and he was the first of the two to land a Winston Cup ride.

But just when his career was on the verge of taking off, it crashed. Alexander was running the Snowball Derby in Pensacola, Fla., one winter when he was involved in a serious wreck. He suffered a devastating head injury that terminated his NASCAR career.

Alexander returned home to Franklin, where he began working in his family's automobile business and pondering what might have been.

"Sure, I often think about where I might be today if I hadn't got hurt, how different my life might have been," Alexander says." But it doesn't do any good to dwell on it. I have been blessed with a good life and a wonderful family, and who knows how things would have turned out if I had kept racing?

"They say that God has a plan for all of us. So who can say that I got a bad break? If I'd been able to keep racing would I be as happy as I am today? I guess we'll never know, will we?"

"Mike was a heckva race driver," Marlin says. "There was no question that he'd have made it big in Winston Cup if he hadn't got hurt. I sure hated it, because I know how much he loved it. It makes me appreciate more what I've been able to do, because I realize that it can all be taken away in a flash."

Indeed, Marlin's own career was interrupted in the 2002 season when a crash at Kansas Speedway left him with two fractured neck vertebrae. He was forced to sit out the final seven races of the season, after leading the championship points standing for 25 consecutive races. What had been shaping up as his best shot at his first Winston Cup championship suddenly was over.

As he said, it can all be gone in a flash.

When Sterling won the '94 Daytona 500, Alexander was watching at home on TV.

"Nobody was cheering louder for Sterling than I was," he said. "I was so thrilled and happy for him. I knew how long and how hard he had worked to get there. I was proud of him. I wish I could have been there with him that day. I guess, maybe in a way, I was."

***

During his days at the Fairgrounds, Marlin raced under two different names. Sometimes he spelled his name "Sterling" and sometimes "Sterlin." Once he showed up for a race with "Sterling" painted on his car and "Sterlin" stitched on his uniform.

I asked him which was the proper spelling.

"Aw, I don't know," he said. "Spell it however you want it. It don't matter to me."

I spelled his name "Sterlin" as it was pronounced. The afternoon paper, the *Nashville Banner*, spelled it "Sterling."

I wrote a story about Marlin's confusing name game: "To g or not to g, that is the question."

Sterling's mom, Eula Faye, failed to see the humor in the situation. She called Joe Caldwell, the *Banner* racing writer, and me, and laid down the law.

"I'm tired of seeing his name spelled two different ways in the newspapers," she said. "People are going to think we're crazy, that we don't even know how to spell our own names. From now on I want it spelled 'Sterling,' like it is on his birth certificate."

And that was that.

***

Eula Faye monitored every story written about her son, and she could be a tough literary critic.

I once wrote a story comparing Sterling's early racing career to that of Kyle Petty's. Kyle, like Sterling, was just getting started in the sport. Kyle's famous father, Richard, was on his way to a record 200th victory; Sterling's dad Coo Coo had never won a big-time race.

I called my story "The Prince and the Pauper."

The phone rang early the next morning. Eula Faye was sputtering on the other end.

"How dare you call Sterling a 'Pauper'?" she snapped. "We may not be as rich and famous as the Pettys, but we're certainly not a bunch of paupers! You're going to have people thinking that we're a bunch of poor hillbillies!"

When she paused for breath, I explained to Eula Faye that the story was not intended to be condescending. It was merely a play on the famous Mark Twain novel, and, she had to admit, Kyle and Sterling WERE coming into the sport from vastly different directions.

Eula Faye gradually calmed down, but not before issuing a stern warning for me to be more careful about what I wrote about her son in the future. She would be reading carefully.

***

Eula Faye was always the mother hen, nervous about her only child's career choice.

She grudgingly tolerated him whizzing around the little Fairgrounds track, where the speeds were relatively slow and safe. But Sterling had his eye on bigger things, at bigger places—like Talladega. The 2.6-mile superspeedway is NASCAR's biggest, fastest, most treacherous track. And it was at Talladega that Sterling was determined to race one summer in an ARCA event.

Sterling and Coo Coo had prepared the car, filed the entry, got everything all set for the race that weekend. Just one problem: how to break the news to Eula Faye. That evening, as the family sat around the dinner table, Coo Coo cleared his throat and said, "Uh, pass the potatoes Sterling's racing at Talladega."

Sterling chuckles at the memory.

"It took about a minute for it to sink in, and then when mama realized what he'd said, sure enough, she hit the ceiling. She started fussin' and sputterin' and carryin' on, just like we knew she'd do. She was dead set against me going to Talladega. But eventually she gave up and gave in; I reckon she knew she didn't have much choice. But she sure wasn't none too happy about it."

***

If Sterling got his determination from his father, he inherited his mother's wit. Eula Faye managed to see the humor in most any situation, even those in which she was the butt of the joke.

One summer at Talladega she was the designated driver after a night on the town with Coo Coo and his old pal, Hoss Ellington.

Hoss had a flashy new Cadillac, fully loaded with all the latest gadgets and gizmos. On the way back to the hotel as she steered the large, unfamiliar car back along a winding road, Eula Faye was pulled over by Talladega police.

With blue lights pulsating ominously in the background, the cop approached the car and tapped on the window with his nightstick. Eula Faye couldn't find the window handle! Hoss, giggling, informed her that it was electric-powered; just push the button, he said.

Frantically, Eula Faye stabbed at a button. The headlights began to flash on and off. She pressed another one. The radio antenna began to go up and down.

The cop tapped again. He was not amused. Poor Eula Faye tried another button. The hood popped up. Now Hoss and Coo Coo were howling with laugher. Finally, desperately, Eula Faye hit the correct button and the window whirred down.

"I was scared to death and almost in tears, the cop was furious because he thought I was acting smart with him, and Coo Coo and Hoss were dying laughing," Eula Faye recalled. "I told the policeman he'd better go ahead and arrest me, because if he didn't I was going to kill the two smart alecks in the car with me!"

The sympathetic cop let Eula Faye proceed on her way.

***

Sterling broke into Winston Cup rich in talent but poor in luck. Time after time he appeared to be in position to win, with victory tingling at his fingertips, only to have it snatched away at the last moment.

Remember the Greek myth about Tantalus, from whom originated the word "tantalize?" The gods punished Tantalus for some transgression by dooming him to forever stand chin-deep in a cool stream, parched with thirst. Each time he bent his head to get a drink, the water would recede just beyond his lips. Sterling was NASCAR's Tantalus; as thirsty as he was for a win, the waters of victory always receded just beyond his reach.

A typical hard-luck story: in a race at Bristol, Marlin had a strong run going and appeared on his way to a win when he ducked into the pits for a final routine stop. A crewman failed to get the lug nuts on. As Marlin roared back onto the track, his right-side tires popped off.

Another time at Bristol, Marlin was leading the race in the closing laps when he was tagged from behind by Dale Earnhardt and sent spinning into the wall. Next day I asked Sterling's dad what he thought about the move by Earnhardt.

"Somebody ought to take him out behind the barn and beat the hell out of him," growled Coo Coo.

It was at Bristol that Marlin had his closest brush with calamity. He was sailing through the second turn one afternoon when his car suddenly swerved out of control and smacked hard into the wall. A fuel line ruptured and in a flash the cockpit was engulfed in flames. As the crowd gasped in horror, Sterling frantically clawed his safety harness loose, wriggled through the window, and collapsed on the ground.

"Everything happened in a split second," Marlin said. "One minute I'm racing along and everything's fine; the next second, wham! I'm in the wall and fire is everywhere. I had the presence of mind not to inhale the flames; that's the biggest danger when you're caught in a fire. I held my breath while I unhooked the safety belts and got the heck out of there."

Marlin suffered second- and third-degree burns on his hands, face and shoulder. He was rushed to a Bristol-area hospital for emergency treatment, then transported to the Vanderbilt Burn Center in Nashville for more specialized care.

When his wife Paula arrived at the hospital, Sterling was wrapped in bandages, his face puffy and swollen. As shaken and terrified as Paula was, she was relieved to learn that her husband's injuries were not life-threatening. She managed to keep her sense of humor.

"Paula walked in, took one look at me, and said, 'You look like you just lost a fight with George Foreman,'" Sterling recalled with a chuckle. "I told her I sure felt like it."

***

Marlin, despite his severe burns, was determined not to miss the next race on the schedule. He checked himself out of the Burn Center and flew to the race with a medical escort. He started the race, wrapped like a mummy in sterile gauze, then came into the pits and turned the car over to a relief driver. He boarded a waiting plane and was whisked back to the Burn Center.

I called Sterling's room shortly after he had been admitted to check on his condition. I expected a nurse or attendant to answer. Instead, Sterling himself picked up the phone. I asked how he was doing.

"Aw, I'm OK," he said. "Heck, I've been sunburned worse than this."

Today Sterling still bears the faint scars from that "sunburn" that he so casually shrugged off.

Finally the determination and perseverance paid off. After 17 years and 278 starts, Sterling found himself in Victory Circle; and not just any Victory Circle, but the Daytona 500. He had reached the Mecca of stock car racing. He had at long last captured racing's Holy Grail. And the Marlin name was engraved on it.

***

Having proved he could win races, Marlin's next goal was to prove he could win championships.

He made a good run in 2001, finishing third behind Jeff Gordon and Tony Stewart. He came out smoking in 2002, winning two of the first three races and leading the points for 25 straight races before his neck injured ended the run. What had been shaping up as his best run at the title ended in bitter disappointment.

"I'll be back," he vowed. "I've got three, four, maybe more good years left, maybe more. I ain't giving up. I know I can do it."

Nobody should doubt him. Remember, he's Coo Coo's son. Bulldog runs in the family.

***

Sports Illustrated ran a lengthy feature on Marlin during his hot run in the 2002 season. The angle *SI* took was that Marlin was part of a vanishing breed in NASCAR—the last of the Good Ol' Boys, men who wound their way into racing from the mills and farms and factories, from the hills of Tennessee, the mountains of the Carolinas, from the red dirt of Georgia and Alabama.

There aren't many of them still around today in Winston Cup, fast-driving, slow-talking Sons of the South. Marlin is one of the enduring—and endearing—ones.

"I've chopped tobacco and shoveled manure and hauled hay until I thought my back was going to break," Sterling says. "I grew up on a farm, working alongside Daddy from sunrise to sunset. It's kinda funny; when I was growing up, I couldn't wait to get away. Now as I grow older I like to go back and putter around the farm."

Marlin is not returning to his roots. He never really left them. He remains unaffected by his wealth and celebrity. He is, as one back-home buddy put it, "as country as corn bread."

He never puts on airs. With Sterling Marlin, what you see is what you get: a genuine Good Ol' Boy, shrugging off setbacks and hard times, forging ahead. Hanging on and hanging in. Just like his daddy taught him.

LAP VI:

FLASH GORDON, WONDER BOY

Jeff Gordon is a young, handsome, charismatic, wealthy national sports celebrity with the world in his palm. Sometimes I pity him.

I get the feeling that Gordon has never had much of a life outside of racing. It seems it is all he has ever known, all he has ever done, and all he was ever prepared to do. When I look at Gordon I sense I am seeing the equivalent of the famous "Bubble Boy" who was forced by illness to remain insulated from the outside world.

Perhaps a better analogy: Jeff at times seems to be the human equivalent of a thoroughbred race horse that has been carefully nurtured and groomed and trained with one purpose in life, and only one: to race.

Allow me to issue this disclaimer: I don't know Gordon personally. Over the years I have been around him many times in public settings, at racetracks, at press conferences, at victory celebrations. I feel that I am well acquainted with the public Jeff Gordon, the racer.

The private Jeff Gordon, the person, is more of a mystery. Almost everyone in the sport knows Gordon the race driver; I don't know anyone who claims to really know Gordon the person.

All of those public encounters are revealing because of what they fail to reveal. Gordon is extremely protective of his privacy, his personal life. Often after one of his many victories or his four Winston Cup championships, he would be asked the standard winner's question:

"Jeff, how do you plan to celebrate?"

Usually his answer would be something along the line of, "Oh, probably just go home, order a pizza, watch some TV and play video games."

You are tempted to shout, "Get a life, Jeff! There is a big, exciting world out there. Kick the door open and barge in. Grab a piece of it. Kick up your heels. Live a little."

But the only thing that seems to grab Gordon's interest is racing. He is immersed in it, consumed by it, possessed by it. He eats it, talks it, and sleeps it. I suspect he dreams about it. And one other thing: he is tremendously good at it.

A strong argument could be made that Jeff Gordon is the best NASCAR driver in history. No driver has won more races and more championships quicker than Gordon. Not Richard Petty. Not Dale Earnhardt. Nobody.

Gordon is an exceptionally talented young man with deep religious convictions who never makes waves. He is unfailingly pleasant and polite. He quietly goes about his business, bothering no one, keeping his nose clean, just doing his job.

So why are all those people booing?

***

There are a lot of theories about why so many NASCAR fans dislike Jeff Gordon.

For starters, he's not "one of them." In fact, he is the antithesis of the prototype Good Ol' Boy. He is a California native whose family moved to Indiana when he was young to further his racing opportunities. He doesn't hunt or fish. I've never heard him discuss football or any other sport other than racing. He doesn't drink, he doesn't smoke, he doesn't cuss. At least not in public. And never in the behind-the-scenes occasions when I've been around him.

I'm often asked if Gordon really is as nice a guy in private as he come across in public. The answer is yes. From what I've observed and from what I've been told by others close to him, yes, he really is that nice of a guy.

Once after a win at Daytona in which Gordon had banged into Dale Earnhardt in the closing laps, I rode the elevator down from the press box with Gordon and then-wife Brooke. Just the three of us, the elevator operator and a security officer assigned to escort the Gordons out.

I heard Jeff whisper to Brooke: "Was Dale mad? What did he say?"

Brooke: "I don't know. I didn't hear him say anything."

Jeff: "Gosh, I sure hope he's not mad at me."

Yes, he really said "gosh."

***

The two top racers in the 1990s were Jeff Gordon and Dale Earnhardt. They were not merely racetrack rivals; they seemed to come from different planets.

Gordon and Earnhardt represented two contrasting worlds, and they were destined to collide. Gordon exuded California cool, the New Generation. Earnhardt was Old School, the son of gritty racer Ralph Earnhardt. Earnhardt was country-hewn and mill-town tough. While Gordon was playing video games, Earnhardt was hunkered down in a deer stand or a bass boat.

Earnhardt ribbed Gordon relentlessly. He called him "Flash Gordon" and "Wonder Boy." Earnhardt wondered if when Gordon won the championship would they serve milk at the NASCAR Awards Banquet?

Gordon did win the title, and when he walked to the podium to make his victory speech, he toasted Earnhardt with a glass of milk. Earnhardt laughed and saluted him back. As different as they were, they shared a mutual respect for each other's tremendous racing talent.

***

Gordon's penchant for wearing his religion on his sleeve turns some fans off.

Invariably after a race Gordon will "thank the Good Lord for a safe day," or "thank God for being with me today." He is not the only driver or the only athlete to recite that sort of testimonial, understand, but it sounds different somehow coming from Gordon. It sounds like he means it.

So that's the rap on Gordon, genuinely a nice guy with deep religious convictions?

One of Gordon's biggest defenders ever since he has been in the sport has been Darrell Waltrip. Maybe it's because Waltrip, more than any other driver, can empathize with him; during his early days in NASCAR no driver was booed more ruthlessly and ferociously than was Waltrip. He knows the sting.

But, Waltrip says, there is a difference between what he went through then and what Gordon is forced to endure now.

"In my case, I asked for a lot of what I got," he says. "I did a lot of controversial stuff back then, said some fairly controversial things, butted heads with a lot of people. I played the role of the villain and I rubbed fans the wrong way. That's why they got onto me so bad. I brought it on myself."

Waltrip pauses, frowns, and continues.

"But that's not the case with Gordon. He hasn't done a thing—not one darned thing—to deserve the kind of treatment he gets from fans. When I hear them booing and hollering ugly stuff at him, it makes me absolutely furious. It makes my blood boil. It makes me wonder sometimes: what kind of people are they, anyway? Gordon is a genuinely good person, a great role model for young people, and for some reason they seem to hate him for it. You wonder what society is coming to."

Publicly, Gordon claims the boos don't bother him.

"Aw, they're just being race fans," he says. "I don't take it personally."

Privately, however, it has to pain and irritate him, just as Waltrip after years of similar denial admitted that the boos hurt, the jeers stung, as they rained down on him unmercifully before and after every race.

Don't misunderstand; Gordon has plenty of fans as well as plenty of detractors. In fact, I'd guess that in recent years he as been the second most popular driver in NASCAR. He trailed Dale Earnhardt when Earnhardt was alive, and now I think he trails Dale Earnhardt, Jr.

Forget that absurd "Most Popular Driver Award" won by Bill Elliott every year. It's absolutely meaningless, except to indicate how loyal and active is Elliott's fan club, which votes early and often in the "Most Popular" balloting.

You want a real indicator of a driver's popularity? Go to a race and check out the percentage of fans wearing his apparel. Dale Jr. and Gordon are in a league all by themselves in the telling Merchandising Poll.

So where do all the boos resonate from?

Simple. Gordon is like the late Howard Cosell, who once was named the most popular sports announcer and the most detested sports announcer in the same year. Put 150,000 fans in the grandstands and even if half of them cheer Gordon, that leaves 75,000 to boo. Boo they do, and 75,000 boo-birds can make a lot of noise.

***

Early in the 2002 season something happened that changed Gordon's image dramatically: he got a divorce.

Brooke, his wife of seven years, filed the papers, citing "marital misconduct."

The Perfect Marriage—the former beauty queen and the handsome race driver—had not been so perfect after all. This wasn't just any split; it was Barbie dumping Ken. It was NASCAR's version of Camelot. And suddenly it was over.

The dirt-digging tabloids had a field day as divorce lawyers mud-wrestled over who got what from the lavish Gordon estate worth an estimated $50 million.

Gordon remained cool amid the chaos that rocked his closely guarded personal life. He issued a brief statement saying that the marriage was over and asking that the press and public respect his privacy during this difficult period. For the most part he got his wish; the only time the media made an issue of the divorce was when his previously brilliant racing performance showed signs of slippage.

The obvious question, and a fair one: Jeff, has the divorce distracted you from racing?

At first he said no, that he was able to separate his personal life from his professional duties, and that when he got to the track and climbed into his car he was as focused and dialed in as ever. Later on, however, he hinted that the marital mess had indeed taken his mind off his driving.

"It had to," Waltrip said. "Jeff is human, just like the rest of us. A divorce has to be one of the most difficult things to happen to anyone.

"When I was racing I needed to be completely focused on what I was doing. I couldn't go to bed at night worrying about something else. A driver's life is all about routine—doing specific things in a specific way at a specific time. Your personal life is part of that routine. Any disruption there causes a disruption to your racing. It's unavoidable."

***

I was struck by what Darrell told me that day:

"Jeff is human."

The public perception had always been that Gordon was some sort of perfect person with a perfect life, and suddenly it was made apparent that that was not the case.

Jeff Gordon, the wealthy superstar, had some of the same problems, troubles, aggravations and headaches as Joe Six Pack. He isn't made of plastic. In the wake of Gordon's divorce, a lot of fans began to look at him in a different light.

Prior to the spring race at Bristol, I decided to talk to some fans to see how their opinion of Gordon might have changed. I wandered through the camping area, stopping to chat with fans at random. Well, not entirely at random. I was especially interested in the views of fans that flew the banners of the Earnhardts, Senior and Junior, since they always seemed to be the toughest on Gordon.

A few told me that their dislike of Gordon was not tempered in the least. He was still too much of "pretty boy," in the words of one grizzled beer gut. "Jeffy" hadn't paid his dues. He was too preppy. He wasn't "one of us."

But others admitted they saw Gordon in a different light in the wake of his divorce.

"I never thought I'd say this, but me and Gordon have got something in common," drawled a scrawny thirty-something who wore his No. 8 cap turned backwards, a la Little E. "My old lady dumped me, too."

He grinned a wry grin and added: "'Course the difference is that Jeff lost a big old mansion. Me, I lost a damn house trailer."

I heard that a lot, from the Good Ol' Boys hunkered down around their smoldering campfires, soaking up beer, barbecue and Hank Williams Jr. ballads.

A mansion on the hill really isn't that much different from a doublewide at the trailer park. D-I-V-O-R-C-E, as Tammy Wynette used to sing, is not picky about addresses.

If Gordon needed a shoulder to cry on, there were plenty available. Women, especially, seemed sympathetic.

"That Brooke is nothing but a gold-digger," was a recurrent theme.

"Jeff risked his life to win all that money," was another. "What did Brooke do? Stood by his side and smiled for the cameras."

"I feel sorry for Gordon," said one willowy young woman with a mane of yellow hair and a skimpy halter-top, as she fired up a Winston. "I think he's kinda naive. He probably ain't been around much. I doubt that he knew what he was getting into. He fell for the wrong gal."

She exhaled a cloud of smoke and smiled a sad smile. "Jeffy got hisself a good, hard, kick in the ass, didn't he?"

Brooke, in fairness, had her defenders.

"She had to have had something on him," opined a middle-aged matron as she scrambled a plate of eggs over a propane grill. "Looks like Mr. Goody-Goody may not have been so good after all."

"Maybe so," grunted her husband as he sipped a breakfast beer from a nearby lawn chair. "But hell, Carlene, you still gotta feel for the guy!"

***

When Jeff Gordon burst onto the NASCAR scene and began dominating races, some felt that he was overrated as a driver, despite his amazing success. Detractors claimed that the man who really deserved the credit was Gordon's crew chief, Ray Evernham.

"Put any other driver out there in Evernham's cars and he can do what Gordon is doing," was a common litany.

Gordon contributed to the perception by always being careful to include Evernham's contributions in his victory speeches. After most wins Evernham would accompany Gordon to the traditional postrace interview session. Sometimes it seemed as though Evernham had won the race and Gordon was merely some spare part that Evernham, the mechanical genius, had installed in the car.

I never bought it. I never thought that Gordon was riding Evernham's coattails to stardom—rather, just the opposite.

I thought then—and still think—that Evernham was fortunate to have hooked up with one of most talented young drivers ever to enter the sport.

As far as I'm concerned, Evernham was just the caddy that handed Gordon his club.

Gordon proved that when Evernham departed to form his own team. Jeff kept right on winning. He even captured another Winston Cup championship, sans Evernham. Wonder how the skeptics explain that?

Meanwhile Evernham, the so-called mechanical mastermind behind Gordon's success, has struggled as a team owner. Somehow Ray's cars don't seem to go quite so fast without Gordon in them, or visit Victory Circle nearly so often.

Although I considered Evernham overrated in terms of his contributions to Gordon's success, I liked him personally. He seemed a pleasant and personable guy, straightforward and honorable—even if he did flit around the spotlight a tad too much at times.

I lost a lot of that respect because of the way he handled Casey Atwood.

Atwood, a bright young driver from Nashville, could have had his pick of Winston Cup rides. Evernham talked Atwood into signing with him as a teammate of Bill Elliott's. Evernham promised Atwood that he would be brought along slowly, allowed to develop at his own pace, with no pressure to perform immediately.

In less than one full season, Ray seemed to change the rules. Toward the end of Atwood's rookie season Evernham announced plans to put Jeremy Mayfield in Atwood's car and relegate Casey to a new third car co-owned by Jim Smith. Atwood's confidence was shattered by the demotion, and he wobbled through a miserable sophomore season. At the end he was let go.

"Ray screwed Casey," said Bobby Hamilton, a veteran driver who had been Atwood's close friend and racing mentor.

"Casey didn't deserve the treatment he received."

Toward the end of the 2002 season, with rumors swirling about a possible Evernham/Atwood split, I attempted to interview Evernham in the garage at Talladega. Evernham exploded and stormed away.

Back to Gordon: Evernham's lackluster results as a team owner reinforced my original opinion that it was Gordon who made Evernham look good, not the other way around. Gordon got where he is today—at the pinnacle of the sport—not because of some fancy wrench turner, but because of his tremendous driving ability.

***

It's hard to stay on the top for long in NASCAR.

Richard Petty enjoyed perhaps the longest run of any driver, but eventually even the great King Richard had to vacate the throne. Today the competition gets tougher every year, the wins harder and harder to come by. Not even Earnhardt could dominate forever.

How long will Gordon endure?

I think he has several better, championship-potential seasons ahead of him. Gordon is young, fresh, and energetic and has managed to avoid serious injury. Exactly how many years he elects to race depends to a great extent on Gordon's desire, on how badly he wants to continue.

Gordon's divorce seemed to bring him out of his shell, to make him more open. Perhaps he will discover that there is a big, fascinating world waiting out there beyond the racetrack. Someday Gordon may decide to unbuckle his helmet and go explore it.

LAP VII:

IT AIN'T BRAGGING IF YOU DO IT

I have often reminded Darrell Waltrip that his racing career didn't take off until I started writing about him. Waltrip, in turn, insists that if it hadn't been for him providing me great stories over the years, I'd probably be covering bowling right now.

The truth of the matter is that we aided and abetted each other's careers, especially in the early going. Waltrip steamrolled into Nashville in the late 1960s from his home in Owensboro, Ky., to hone his racing skills at the historical old Fairgrounds track. He had outgrown the little bullrings sprinkled throughout the Bluegrass. He migrated to the Music City in search of greater challenges, to fulfill a destiny that he was convinced held fame and fortune.

I arrived in Nashville about the same time to attend college and landed a part-time job at *The Nashville Tennessean* sports department. One of my earliest assignments was covering racing as a backup for our regular beat writer.

I quickly learned that if you needed a good story, talk to Waltrip. You didn't have to look for him; he'd find you. Back then, Darrell sought out publicity like a beagle sniffs out rabbits in a brush pile.

Waltrip was brash and brazen, cocky and confident. He was always fanning the fames of some controversy, stirring up trouble, gouging at the Good Ol' Boy regulars at the track.

He drove like he talked: fast and furious, never backing off or backing down. He was by far the best driver ever to come through Nashville. If you didn't believe it, just ask him.

"Boys, it ain't bragging if you can do it," Waltrip liked to say. "I'm just telling it like it is."

"Telling it like it is" caused one of my rare squabbles with Waltrip.

It all started one summer when a kid named Gary Adams kept running away with the races in a lower division. The track promoter, Bill Donoho, called Adams into his office one night after yet another boring blowout and "suggested" that he back off a little. Donoho told Adams to let some of the other drivers hang with him up front a little, make a better show of it. In other words, stop racing so hard. Adams told Donoho he wouldn't do it.

Donoho told Adams that if he didn't, he would be suspended. Adams phoned me at the newspaper and told me about Donoho's threat. He said Donoho came dangerously close to ordering him to "fix" a race.

I called Donoho to get his side of the story. He insisted there was nothing wrong with what he told Adams—"slow down a little and stop stinking up the show." "Hell fire," Donoho thundered, "I told Waltrip to do the same thing lots of times, and he did."

Let me get this straight, I said: Darrell Waltrip, at your instruction, intentionally slowed down to make his races appear closer than they really were?

"Damn right, he did," Donoho said.

I called Waltrip and told him what Donoho had told me. Well? What did he have to say?

"Yeah, I did it a few times," Waltrip said.

"So what? Why run your car in the ground if you don't have to? Why wear out your equipment? It's like sending the subs in the fourth quarter when you've got a big lead in a football game. If you've got a big lead in the race why not back off a little and play with the field a little bit? Makes it more interesting for the fans."

I had my big "expose:" ace driver Darrell Waltrip admitted that he at times ran "fake speeds" at the behest of the track promoter to make races appear closer and more exciting than they really were, and that some of his "dramatic finishes" were merely contrived to thrill the fans.

My phone jangled early the next morning.

"You made me look like an idiot!" boomed Waltrip. "I tried to level with you, to explain how things work in this sport, and you turned everything around and made me look stupid. Now the fans are mad at me and the drivers are mad at me—they'll think I've just been playing with them out there. Don't you ever call me again for another story!"

Bam!

Donoho wasn't angry; he loved controversy because it meant publicity. Waltrip eventually cooled down. He loved publicity, too.

***

The truth of the matter was that Waltrip indeed *was* often toying with the local competition; he was that much better than most of his rivals. It didn't take him long to spread his racing wings, and he plowed into NASCAR's big leagues with the same reckless abandon and magnum force with which he had hit Nashville Speedway.

Waltrip was about as subtle as a runaway locomotive. Nobody in the sport's history had walked the walk and talked the talk the way Darrell did. Nobody had ever dared to refer to venerable NASCAR president Bill France, Sr., as "our Great White

Darrell Waltrip is buckled in and awaiting the start of a race.

Father in Daytona." Waltrip did, once, when peeved over some uncompromising decree issued by NASCAR with which he disagreed.

Most drivers just fumed and muttered when they didn't like something NASCAR did; Waltrip shouted from the rooftops. He aggravated and agitated NASCAR so much during his rookie season that the then-subjective Winston Cup Rookie of the Year Award was bestowed on humble, make-no-waves Lennie Pond, even though gadfly Waltrip had a much superior season.

Being portrayed as the sport's resident bad boy, an early-day John McEnroe on wheels, didn't bother Waltrip in the least. In fact, he seemed to relish his rebel image. He continued to gouge the NASCAR establishment and thumb his nose at the sport's resident heroes like Richard Petty and David Pearson.

Cale Yarborough nicknamed Waltrip "Jaws," after the shark in the popular movie of the period.

"Waltrip runs his mouth all the time and chews up everything that gets in his way on a racetrack," Cale growled.

Fans booed Waltrip at every stop. They jeered when he won and cheered when he lost. I asked Darrell if the slings and arrows that rained down on him stung.

"Naaa," he said "I'm just stirring the pot a little. Making things interesting. Giving you guys something to write about."

Later in his career, Waltrip admitted there was method to his madness.

"I realized early on that to succeed in this sport you've gotta get noticed," he explained.

"And the best way for a kid from Nashville with no big name to get noticed was to create a little controversy. That's how you got your name in the papers, how you got people to pay attention to you.

"I discovered that if I said something fairly outrageous, the next day it would be in the papers. Never mind that ol' Richard won another race—man, look what that crazy Waltrip said! It's like Bill Donoho used to say: there ain't no such thing as bad publicity. There's just publicity."

Waltrip compared himself to Jack Nicklaus: "When Nicklaus began beating Arnold Palmer, everybody's favorite golfer, the galleries booed him. Same with me. I came in and started beating Petty and Pearson and all the good old boy favorites, and a lot of the fans didn't like it. Well, to heck with the fans. They might as well get used to it, 'cause I'm gonna be beating those dudes for a long time to come."

***

Joe Carver was the Speedway's PR director when Waltrip arrived in Nashville. Carver eventually quit his job and went to work for Darrell. He ran errands, helped set up media interviews, scheduled PR appearances, chauffeured Waltrip around, and handled other assorted odd jobs.

I once asked Waltrip what, exactly, was Carver's title.

"Slave," Darrell quipped.

Carver was devoted to Waltrip, and privately worried about him. "Darrell's really a sensitive guy deep down," Joe told me once. "He puts on this tough, macho act in public, but it really hurts him when the fans boo him like that. I think it's starting to get to him."

Waltrip likewise couldn't hide his true feelings from wife Stevie. "The people who boo Darrell don't know him," she said. "They don't realize that most of the stuff he does is just some silly act. When they boo it hurts him, and it hurts me to see him hurt. I can't tell you how many times I've left a track in tears."

Eventually, as Carver predicted, it did get to Waltrip. One year at Charlotte (now Lowe's Motor Speedway), Waltrip was involved in a hard crash. As safety workers removed him from his mangled car, barely conscious, Waltrip heard the roar of the crowd over the ringing in his ears.

"Suddenly it hit me—they were cheering!" Waltrip said. "Cheering! There I was, on a stretcher being loaded into an ambulance, and they were on their feet cheering! I could have been hurt bad, even killed, and those stupid idiots were cheering their heads off. It makes you question the mentality of race fans. I'm ashamed of them. I wouldn't want my kids sitting in the stands with sick morons like that. I'm about to the point of going out and posting notices on light poles around the track: Any SOB who don't like me can meet me in the parking lot at K-Mart and we'll duke it out."

I wrote the story and it moved nationally on the Associated Press sports wire:

"Furious Waltrip Invites Fans to Duke it Out!"

***

It was along about then that Waltrip began to realize that he had, indeed, created a monster, and that the monster had gotten out of control and run amok. It was time to undergo an image transplant.

"I've gotta get this situation under control," he told me. "I love this sport and I want to make a contribution to it. I don't want to be remembered like this."

Waltrip set out to mend his public relations fences and create a new image—kinder, gentler. He toned down the rhetoric, took fewer potshots at his rivals. He was more humble in victory and less contentious in defeat.

It worked. Gradually fans began to see a different Darrell. They saw more wit and less malice. The boos began to die. Not overnight, but eventually. The transformation was complete when one season Waltrip was voted Most Popular Driver.

Finally, after all the years of feuds, fireworks and firefights, Waltrip was no longer the driver the fans most loved to loathe.

***

I was at Daytona one summer for the Firecracker 400, and after the morning practice session was about over I returned to the motel to write.

A few minutes later after I got there, the phone rang. It was Jim Freeman, the Daytona Speedway PR director with whom I'd

*Darrell Waltrip holds up one of the
84 trophies he won during his career.*

been friends for years. Freeman started out as sports information director at Middle Tennessee State University in Murfreesboro, and he knew that anything involving Waltrip was an important story for me.

"Woodrow," Freeman said, "bad news. Waltrip just crashed in practice and they've taken him to a local hospital. Looked pretty bad. You might want to get back over here."

I hurried back to the track, wondering how Waltrip could have crashed. He had finished his practice session before I left. Freeman explained that Waltrip had decided to go back out for a few more laps, and that's when the crash occurred.

For the rest of the afternoon and through most of the night I monitored Waltrip's hospital status and filed updated stories to the paper. The most serious of Darrell's injuries was a broken left femur, the large bone in his upper leg. Waltrip left the hospital a few days later, wearing a cast up to his hip.

The next race was at Pocono, Pa., and Waltrip, on crutches, vowed that he was going to run it. I went to Pocono and watched from pit road as Waltrip's crew loaded him into his car through the window like a sack of potatoes, his face twisted in pain. He ran a few laps (to get credit in the points standings for the car's finish), and then came in to be hauled back out through the window.

It hurt to watch.

Waltrip was tough. In one of his Grand National races at Nashville his crew left a heat shield out of the floorboard of his car. His heel was burned so badly that the bone was charred and required a bone graft. Waltrip said that about midway through the race he could smell his flesh burning.

Why didn't he come in?

"I was leading," he said.

After another race on a hot muggy night, Waltrip was so exhausted that he almost fainted. He had to conduct his postrace interview lying on his back, wearing an oxygen mask.

He won that race, too.

***

Waltrip has a mischievous streak in him and can be a wicked prankster.

We had breakfast together once while at an out-of-town race, and Darrell was constantly interrupted by autograph seekers. Even the waitress and the restaurant manager asked for his signature.

Finally, Darrell said he had to get going. I, meanwhile, was in no hurry; I told him I was going to finish my coffee and newspaper. I'd see him later at the track. Waltrip picked up the check—a first, I reminded him—and strolled to the counter to pay the bill.

He chatted with our waitress and the manager for a moment, and I noticed they seemed to be cutting glances back at me. Shortly afterwards I decided to head out. As I walked by the checkout counter I could tell the waitress and manager were eyeballing me.

"Everything OK?" I said. "Did Darrell leave the gratuity?"

"Oh, yes sir! Everything's fine sir!" said the manager. "Mr. Waltrip took care of everything!"

He appeared nervous. So did the waitress. They kept their eye on me as I walked out the door.

Later, at the track, Waltrip spotted me and walked over, grinning. "So," he said, "did you get out of the restaurant OK?"

I asked him what he meant.

"When I paid the bill I told the manager that he better keep an eye on you," Waltrip said. "I told him that you were some weird old guy who traveled around, impersonating a sports writer so that you could hang around the drivers. I said I felt sorry for you and let you sit with me and even bought you breakfast. I told them that as far as I knew you were basically harmless, but that if I was them I'd keep an eye on you because you ever know when some crazy old dude like you might go completely nuts." He snickered.

"Good thing you didn't make any sudden moves; they might have thrown a net over you."

***

For a span in the early to mid-1980s Darrell Waltrip was the hottest thing on wheels, the best driver in NASCAR, the absolute King of the Road.

The Old Guard was graying—Petty, Pearson, Allison, Yarborough, Baker—and some of the fierce young lions like Dale Earnhardt were just starting to roar. Future superstar Jeff Gordon had barely graduated from go-karts.

Waltrip won three Winston Cup championships and 84 races, and he made it look easy. Then, toward the close of the decade, he made a fatal career decision. He got greedy. He wanted to be the boss as well as the driver. He formed his own team, and his career never recovered.

Burdened by the double duties, the massive responsibilities of overseeing a huge racing operation, Waltrip's driving began to gradually slump. Then it nose-dived, and he never pulled out of the spin.

Waltrip went winless through his final seasons as a racer. Too proud to give up, convinced that he could somehow recapture the old magic, desperately he drove on.

It was sad to watch: Waltrip wobbling around the track, tagging along at the end of the field, failing to qualify for races.

It was like watching a great thoroughbred end his days plodding along as a plow horse. I often asked Darrell why he didn't quit.

"I don't want to get out while I'm on the bottom," he said. "I don't want the fans to remember me like this, especially the new fans who never saw me back when I was winning. All those fans who don't have any concept of the kind of driver I used to be. "

If only he could win just one more race, bask in the warm glow of victory just one more time. It wasn't meant to be. Just as it never happened for Richard Petty, it never happened for Waltrip. They both hung on too long. The sweet serenades of success had seduced them; both tried to keep dancing long after the music stopped.

During Petty's final, futile years, Waltrip told me, "It's so sad to watch Richard like that. Why can't he realize it? Why doesn't someone take him aside and explain to him that it's over, that he needs to hang it up? I guarantee you, I'll never stick around like that."

But he did. Just like nobody had the courage to tell Petty, nobody had the nerve to tap Waltrip on the shoulder and tell him: "Come on, Darrell ... it's time to go."

Finally it ended, on a bright, blustery late-November afternoon at Atlanta Motor Speedway. Darrell ran his final Winston Cup race. I was waiting in his pit area when he pulled off the track for the last time. He came to a stop, took off his helmet, and got a kiss from Stevie. Slowly he climbed from his car.

One of the greatest careers in NASCAR was over. Maybe it was the harsh sunlight that made Darrell's eyes glitter. Maybe it was the stinging wind that caused his eyes to water, sending a single tear coursing down his cheek. Whatever it was, it made my eyes water a little that day, too.

***

Waltrip didn't leave racing. He simply went from driving to analyzing. As soon as he retired at the end of the 2000 season, he was hired by Fox Sports as a color commentator for the network's upcoming new NASCAR broadcasts. Waltrip proved to be a natural in the broadcast boot—glib and quick-witted, smooth and articulate, knowledgeable and perceptive.

Perhaps no single driver did more to change the public's opinion about stock car racers than Waltrip. He came into the sport as a dapper dresser, carefully manicured, sporting sleek razor-haircuts. He was careful with his grammar, neat in word and manner. He was the antithesis of the sport's "redneck" image.

Waltrip proclaimed himself the harbinger of a new age in racing.

"In NASCAR we've gone from having wine *for* our dinner to having wine *with* our dinner," he liked to say. (Actually, he stole that line from one of my columns, but I told him he could use it.)

Waltrip transfers that flair and élan to TV. In his prime there was no better driver on the track; now, in prime time, there is no better announcer.

The engines gurgle to life and Waltrip—D. W. to his legions of fans—delights Fox's millions of viewers with his trademark, "Boggity, boogity, boogity!"

And, once again, the race is on.

***

Waltrip and I had dinner together at a restaurant in Rockingham, N.C., the night after Dale Earnhardt's memorial service, just the two of us, at a quiet booth in the back.

We had attended the service in Charlotte that morning, then motored on over to Rockingham, site of the next race.

We discussed Earnhardt's shocking death at Daytona the week before. It was a somber conversation. We both had been extremely fond of Earnhardt. I was watching from the press box when he crashed. Waltrip was calling the race on TV. He plunged from an absolute high—seeing his younger brother Michael capture his first victory—to an absolute low.

"Boys, I sure hope Dale's OK," Waltrip had said softly, as the telecast ended. Word of Earnhardt's death had not yet been announced. I shared a secret with Waltrip: for 30 years I had lived in trepidation that someday I might have to attend a memorial service for him like the one we had attended that morning for Earnhardt. Waltrip survived some close calls, some frightening moments.

Thankfully, he survived, and I would never have to write the story I had feared someday I might have to write.

Darrell Waltrip and Benny Parsons check out a trophy at North Wilkesboro in the late '70s

Darrell and I grew up in the sport together. We worked together, helped each other, kidded each other, argued at times ... for more than three decades he was my best friend in racing.

He still is.

LAP VIII:

AGGRAVATION IN SMALL DOSES

For 33 years I have interviewed dozens—hundreds, actually—of race drivers.

From the legends of the sport like Richard Petty and A. J. Foyt to nondescript weekend warriors and local wannabes at Nashville Speedway and other little Saturday night bullrings scattered throughout Middle Tennessee, I have dealt with racers on every level of the sport.

I can count on one hand the number of problem drivers I have encountered.

Among the big-leaguers—NASCAR Winston Cup—I don't even need the full hand. Two fingers will suffice. One for Ernie Irvan, one for Tony Stewart. (I'm willing to reserve judgment on Stewart; more on him later.) First Ernie Irvan.

I always admired Irvan's gritty work ethic and his tenacity; he started from scratch and worked tirelessly to make himself into a great racer. I appreciated his determination and his incredible courage. He overcame adversity and injuries, including one near-fatal crash. He endured and raced on when most people would have counted their blessings and walked away.

But despite his triumphs and successes, Ernie always seemed determined to make life difficult, sometimes downright miserable, for those around him. I was not alone in this impression. Many, if not most, of the media who covered NASCAR during Irvan's years in the sport shared similar sentiments. So did many of his fellow drivers, privately. They told me so.

I have never judged drivers or anyone else on their reputation, by what others said or wrote or thought about them (remember Lee Petty?). I have a simple standard: I judge them by how they treat me, and by how I see them treat others around them. Irvan always treated me like dirt.

Once at Indy, while Irvan was sidelined during his recovery from his first serious crash, his teammate at Robert Yates Racing, Dale Jarrett, announced a press conference. It was held in an infield tent. It was packed by media on hand for the big Brickyard bash.

Just before Jarrett and Yates took the stage, Irvan walked in and sat down at a table by himself.

I thought Ernie might make an interesting story. How was his convalescence going? What were his immediate plans? His long-term plans? How was he dealing with being sidelined?

I walked over, introduced myself, and asked how he was feeling.

"How do you think I'm feeling?" he snapped.

I forged ahead. I asked about his medical prognosis.

"Do you ever read the papers?" he said. "That story has been written a hundred times!"

I told him it had not been written by me and had not appeared in my newspaper. I said I thought racing fans in Middle Tennessee would be interested in reading about how he was getting along.

"Look," said Irvan, his voice rising. "I don't want to talk to you people. I wish you'd leave me the hell alone!"

I suppose I should have walked away at that point. But I didn't.

"Well, if you want to be left alone by the media, then why did you show up at a press conference?" I asked.

Irvan stood up and got in my face. His eyes were flashing and his face was beet red.

"I'm telling you for the last time—get the hell away from me and leave me alone!" he snarled.

A crowd began to gather around us. TV cameras started to roll. Quickly, a Yates PR guy stepped in. He took Irvan's arm and steered him away, toward the exit. A few minutes later he returned and began to profusely apology for Irvan's behavior.

"Forget it," I said. "Guess I caught him at a bad time."

"For Ernie, any time is a bad time," the PR guy sighed. "He wasn't invited here. He just showed up. When he walked in I was afraid we'd have a problem. This is not the first time something like this has happened."

***

Another incident, also at Indy: it was midway through Darrell Waltrip's final season and I was doing a story on his fellow drivers' favorite stories about him during his 30-year career. Everybody was willing, even anxious to cooperate.

Ricky Rudd spun his favorite yarn about him and Darrell criss-crossing sponsorship paths during their career.

Benny Parsons told a funny story about getting snookered by Waltrip, who out-foxed him to win a race.

Rusty Wallace invited me into his hauler, where he sat down and told great Waltrip stories for 30 minutes.

I had filled a notebook with terrific anecdotes and was feeling pretty good about the project. It was going to make a terrific story. I was headed back to the Media Center to start writing when I spotted Irvan lounging beside a bay in the garage. He was idly chatting with a member of another pit crew. They were laughing and joking, clearly not immersed in any sort of business discussion.

I walked over. They turned and looked at me. I told Irvan who I was and what I'd like—his favorite story about Darrell Waltrip. It didn't have to be long, just a couple of minutes.

"Not now, I'm busy," Irvan said. He turned to the crewman and grinned.

"Well, when would be a good time?" I asked.

"I don't know—check with my PR guy," Irvan said, adding, "I'm *real* busy right now." Another goofy sophomoric smirk. The crewman snickered.

"OK, where is —"

"Look, buddy, I told you—I'm BUSY!"

The crewman snorted. Irvan grinned at him. They were still grinning and giggling as I walked away.

I wrote one word in my notebook, beside Irvan's name: "Ass!"

One bad encounter, maybe just a bad moment. Two times, screw him.

I went back to the Media Center and wrote a scathing column about what a total jerk Ernie Irvan is. After the column ran nationally I received a letter from Irvan's PR people apologizing—again—for his boorish behavior.

I wondered if the poor PR guy had a stack of form letters for such occasions.

***

Birmingham sports writer Clyde Bolton once had a similar experience with a big-name driver. Bolton was bolder than me. He told the driver, "Look, buddy, if you don't want to talk to me, that's fine. There's 42 other drivers out there. And if they're all as big a prick as you, I'll go home and write about football."

Bolton, one of the sport's most talented and influential writers, never spoke to the driver again.

A couple of years after the Indy incident, Irvan decided to retire. The announcement was made in the Media Center at Bristol Motor Speedway prior to a race. All the press was on hand.

Amid Irvan's goodbye speech, a writer wondered why Ernie was not making a "Farewell Tour" as did Waltrip and Richard Petty during their final seasons.

"In Irvan's case it wouldn't be called a 'Farewell Tour,'" I said. "It would be a 'Goodbye And Good Riddance Tour.'"

Clyde Bolton had the right idea.

Irvan hopes to remain active in the sport as a team owner, and I wish him well. But I won't be writing any stories about him in the near future.

***

Now, Tony Stewart. I don't understand him. I'm not sure that Tony understands Tony a lot of the time.

Handsome, intelligent, articulate, great sense of humor. Immensely talented racer. Stewart won the 2002 Winston Cup championship, adding it to an Indy Racing League title he captured prior to moving to NASCAR—the only driver in history to win both. Stewart is without question one of the most versatile drivers in all of motor sports. Some are already comparing him to the legendary A. J. Foyt.

He is not just a tremendous racing talent. At times Tony Stewart can be one of the most charming, engaging individuals you've ever been around. Other times he can be one of the most irritating.

The problem is, you never know which Tony Stewart is going to show up from day to day. One minute he is joking and smiling; the next minute he is sarcastic, defensive, combative, going out of his way to create conflict and cause trouble.

Stewart was on NASCAR probation when he won the championship. That captures the conflicting Tonys perfectly: a NASCAR champion while on NASCAR probation. The best and the worst, at the same time.

Following the Brickyard 400 at Indy, Stewart struck a photographer for having the audacity to try to take his picture. Stewart's sponsor, Home Depot, was so outraged that it fined him $50,000 and put him on season-long probation—unprecedented in the sport.

Although team owner Joe Gibbs steadfastly stood by his driver, Home Depot made it clear that it could not condone further such behavior.

Later in the season a female fan at Bristol claimed Stewart shoved her down and cursed her. A deputy sheriff said he witnessed the incident and the case went all the way to a Tennessee grand jury before being dropped.

Next, a track safety official claimed Stewart struck him when he tried to help him from his car after a crash. Tapes of the incident suggested it was more of a brushoff than a punch. Even so, it makes Tony look bad, swiping at a safety attendant who was only trying to help him.

The previous season Stewart was put on NASCAR probation not once but twice for bad behavior. It seemed as though he was determined to self-destruct. Stewart admitted he had a problem with his temper. He swore he was trying to get it in check. He retained an "anger management counselor."

***

My personal encounter with Stewart came in the 2001 season following a race at Bristol. Tony won the race after a heated late-race battle with Jeff Gordon. Ironically, the year before, Gordon had won a similar battle with Stewart to win the race. Afterwards an irate Stewart intentionally rammed Gordon's car on pit road, drawing the first of his two NASCAR fines and probations.

After his victory in the return battle, Stewart came to the topside press box for the customary postrace press conference. I asked Tony if the earlier tangle with Gordon had been on his mind during the decisive final laps of their battle.

"Are you a local?" Stewart snapped.

A local what, I wondered?

We exchanged a few more words, then Stewart growled, "Look, if you've got a question I wish you'd go ahead and ask it. I'd like to get out of here sometime tonight!"

"OK," I said, taking a deep breath and speaking slowly into the press box microphone: "Were you thinking about your last race here, when you deliberately ran into Jeff Gordon on pit road after the race and got fined and put on probation?"

Stewart was seething. He is accustomed to intimidating the media, snapping at any question he doesn't like, backing people down. Perhaps for the first time ever, someone was refusing to be bullied and intimidated and stood up to him. He clearly was not used to it.

At that point, with tensions running strong, NASCAR official Danielle Humphrey intervened. She grabbed the microphone away and asked "Any further questions for Tony?"

Someone lobbed him a softball, and he was happy again.

I wrote a column saying that the Hoosier Hothead was destined to do one of two things: become a NASCAR champion (if he learned to behave), or get his butt kicked out of the sport (if he didn't).

The first prediction came true, but not before the second one almost did Tony in.

***

Stewart saw me as the epitome of his perceived "media enemies." He seems convinced that the press is out to get him, to provoke him into doing something stupid and self-destructive. That's not true—I don't know a single writer who deliberately sets out to make Tony look bad.

During a subsequent race at Darlington, *The Tennessean's* music writer, Peter Cooper, attended the race with the country music group Diamond Rio. Diamond Rio was there as Stewart's special guest. When Stewart discovered that Cooper wrote for *The Tennessean*—my paper—he initially balked at allowing him to travel with the party.

Cooper returned and wrote a story about his day at the race with Diamond Rio and included a flattering portrayal of Stewart as his host.

Cooper said he found Tony to be one of the nicest, most pleasant and engaging people he had ever been around. He said he didn't understand why I'd had a problem with him.

I told Peter he was lucky; he had got to see one Tony Stewart. Fortunately for him, he didn't encounter the Other Tony.

As I said, at times Stewart can be gracious and outgoing, with the ability to laugh at himself. After making a fuss over being required to wear a head and neck protective device in 2001 (a new NASCAR safety rule that had to be obeyed by all drivers) Tony showed up at the Winston Cup Awards Banquet in New York wearing one of the devices under his tux.

He did something similar at the 2002 banquet at which he was crowned champion. He produced a camera and playfully began snapping pictures of the photographers—a joke about the run-ins he had had with the shutterbugs during the season.

Stewart once told a magazine writer that the fans at Talladega were the "most obnoxious" in racing, making folks in Alabama furious. Stewart held a press conference with Alabama media, during which he apologized. He said he meant "obnoxious" in a good way.

Later, he showed up at Talladega Superspeedway wearing a T-shirt inscribed

"Obnoxious Talladega Race Driver."

Give Tony credit: he has a sense of humor.

***

Stewart has always been outspoken.

He was the first driver to call attention to the crowded NASCAR garages and prod the governing body to implement some long-overdue restrictions to fan access. I don't mind that. I like drivers who are not afraid to speak their minds on touchy, controversial subjects. Darrell Waltrip did it for decades.

But I don't like drivers who try to bully their way through the sport, drivers who abuse fans, drivers who assault members of the media who are trying to do their jobs. (Stewart once slapped a reporter's tape recorder out of his hand and kicked it away. He later apologized and bought the reporter a new recorder.)

Richard Petty put it best, as Stewart was preparing to put the wraps on his championship going into the final race at Homestead-Miami Speedway:

"If drivers in the past had treated people the way Tony does, he wouldn't be racing for a Winston Cup championship," Petty told Chris Jenkins of *USA Today*, "because there wouldn't be no NASCAR Winston Cup Series."

Petty is correct. The symbiotic relationship between drivers and media, between drivers and fans, which Petty and others like him nurtured over the years, is what made the sport what it is today.

Tony's problem is that he can be spoiled and selfish; he wants to savor and enjoy the pleasures and rewards of racing without having to make any of the sacrifices or endure any of the aggravations.

He needs to learn that life doesn't work that way. It's called "growing up."

After Stewart won the title, he made an emotional postrace speech in which he admitted that his bad behavior and reckless actions "almost tore this team apart." He said he was lucky he had not been fired, been dumped by Home Depot and Joe Gibbs Racing. He said he realized that he was fortunate to still be in NASCAR. He swore that he had learned his lesson with his close call. He vowed to change his ways.

For what it's worth, I thought he sounded sincere. I'm willing to give Tony the benefit of the doubt, a second chance. I hope he is able to clean up his act, because at times he can be enjoyable to work with. He clearly has the talent to become a dominant driver in NASCAR for many years to come.

If, that is, he can conquer the temperamental demons that seem to always squirm and dance just beneath the surface. If the demons win, however, Stewart is doomed. He won't last in the sport.

Tony has proven that he can triumph on the racetrack. But can he triumph over his own soul?

His destiny is in his own hands.

LAP IX:

THE WRECKER DRIVER

Bobby Hamilton says if you think slamming a stock car through heavy traffic at 200 miles per hour is hard, dangerous driving, you ain't seen nothing yet. Try driving a repo wrecker.

That's what Hamilton did for a while as a young man in Nashville, hauling away repossessed vehicles from owners who often didn't stand by idly and allow their possessions to go quietly.

"Man, it could get pretty wild," says Hamilton. "You learned to ease in at night, when they were asleep. Or when they weren't home.

"If they caught you trying to tow away their car, there could be trouble. I've been cussed at, threatened, shot at. Once as I was driving off with a guy's car on the hook, he ran out and jumped on the back of my wrecker. He kicked the rear window out, reached in and got a chain around my neck and tried to choke me.

"When I finally got loose I said, 'Hell, buddy, you can have your damn car back if you want it that bad!'"

Hamilton grew up in East Nashville—the tough, gritty side of town—a product of a broken home. Hamilton's parents divorced when he was 18 months old, and he was sent to live with his grandparents.

A fiercely private man, Hamilton has never been comfortable talking about himself or discussing his family. But one day when I paid a visit to him at his racing shop just outside of town, he sat down and uncharacteristically bared his soul.

I had known Bobby for over 20 years, and that day he shared feelings and sentiments I'd never before heard him express.

"My father was an alcoholic," Hamilton said. "Liquor destroyed his life, ruined our family, and I hate it for what it did. To this day I don't like to be around it. I've seen what it does to people. I never thought my father was a bad person; he just couldn't handle the liquor."

Bobby's grandfather was Charles "Preacher" Hamilton, and he drove race cars. "My daddy was a great racer," says Bobby's aunt, Beverly. "He raced everywhere—at little tracks around Nashville and all over the South. But that was back before racing got much attention, back even before NASCAR was formed, and he never received much credit."

***

Bobby's troubled father, Bud, dabbled briefly in racing, but his main interest lay in the mechanics of the sport, rather than in the driving. He was more at home under the hood than behind the wheel. Bud Hamilton's primary claim to fame was helping Preacher build and maintain the race cars driven by country-western singer Marty Robbins. Bobby inherited the family racing genes.

"Growing up, I was around racing and race cars from the time I could walk," he says. "I liked racing, but I honestly never gave a lot of thought to doing it for a living. Back in them days you couldn't make any money running the local tracks, and Winston Cup—well, that was something that the big-name guys like Richard Petty got to do."

Just for the fun of it, Hamilton began running some Saturday night fender-benders at Highland Rim Speedway, a little quarter-mile track north of Nashville. He did pretty well. So well, in fact, that he decided to try his luck at Nashville Speedway, where the competition was tougher and, on a good night, a driver might be able to pay his gas and tire bill and still walk away with a few dollars in his pocket.

Times were hard in those days. Driving a wrecker didn't pay much. Hamilton recalls one weekend when he was too broke to afford a set of tires for his race car.

"I called my mom and asked her if she could help me out," he says. "Somehow, she came up with the money. I don't know how she did it—maybe went to the bank and borrowed it—but she got it. Back then you literally raced from paycheck to paycheck. You took what you won one weekend and used it to race on the next weekend."

***

Hamilton was good—genetically gifted, perhaps—and as the victories and championships (1987 and 1988) kept piling up at Nashville Speedway, he began to attract attention.

Among the eyes he caught were those of Darrell Waltrip, a former Nashville racer who had graduated up to Winston Cup.

"Darrell had always been my hero in racing," Hamilton says. "I was flattered when he would drop by and talk to me during his visits back to the track. One weekend he had to be out of town for some reason the day before he was scheduled to run a Busch race at the Fairgrounds. Darrell asked me if I would set up his car and qualify it for him. I did, and after the race he told me it was the best-handling car he had ever driven. Coming from Darrell Waltrip, I considered that quite a compliment."

"Bobby was always car-smart," said Waltrip. "I understand that his father and his grandfather were both great racing mechanics, and I guess that's where he learned it. A lot of racers know how to drive a car; not as many know how to set one up. Bobby was good at both."

Waltrip's friendship would eventually provide Hamilton his big career break. Darrell was driving for Rick Hendrick, and Hendrick was acquainted with some of the people involved in producing a racing movie, *Days of Thunder*, starring Tom Cruise. The movie people needed someone to drive a car at Phoenix specifically to provide some film footage. They asked Hendrick if he could recommend someone. Hendrick asked Waltrip, and Waltrip recommended Hamilton.

Hamilton did such a good job driving the "movie car" that he caught the attention of some Winston Cup team owners, and before long he had been offered a ride.

You could say that Bobby Hamilton's rise to racing stardom was literally right out of a Hollywood script.

***

I've been acquainted with Hamilton for over a quarter-century, but I'm not sure I know him that well.

I like him. I admire him. But Hamilton is not the sort who lets people get close to him. Except for that rare moment that afternoon when he sat down and candidly discussed his father's drinking problem and how it devastated his family, Bobby has always kept his private life wrapped in a tight, protective cocoon. The media or other outsiders are seldom able to penetrate it.

I do a Nashville racing radio show twice a week. The host, Carl P. Mayfield, is not only one of the country's top country music personalities, he is also an avid NASCAR fan. We frequently have drivers as guests on the show, but over the years Hamilton has declined repeated invitations.

After his last rejection, I asked him why.

"Aw, I ain't got nothin' to say," Hamilton said. "I always figured that if you ain't got nothin' to say, it's better to just keep your mouth shut."

Most celebrities and star athletes will tell you they don't crave publicity, that they don't warm to the spotlight. They're fibbing. Despite their protests to the contrary, most of them actually do enjoy the attention and adulation.

Not Hamilton. When he says he doesn't care about it, he really means it. I am convinced that he would be perfectly content to race without ever hearing his name mentioned on television, without seeing his picture in the paper.

Bobby Hamilton is one of those rare celebrity moths that has never been drawn to the flame.

***

Hamilton has a reputation among the racing media as a reclusive driver, indifferent to publicity, at times difficult to gain access to and deal with. Dale Earnhardt was the same way in his early years. Earnhardt gradually warmed to the attention; I don't believe Hamilton ever will.

Because he is so intensely private, most folks don't realize that he is a highly sensitive person, keenly intelligent, deeply perceptive, with emotions that he keeps carefully cloaked. When Earnhardt died at Daytona, Hamilton was so distraught that he shut himself off not only from the press and the public, but also from his own family. During the days that followed Earnhardt's death I repeatedly phoned Hamilton's office to seek his reaction to the tragedy. His aunt Beverly, who oversees Hamilton's racing operation, said he had given her strict orders not to take any media calls concerning Earnhardt.

"Bobby's all tore up," Beverly said. "He won't even talk to me about it, and we've been like brother and sister all our lives."

The death of Adam Petty a year before Earnhardt died hit Hamilton equally hard, if not harder. Hamilton once drove for Richard Petty, and has remained close to the family. His son, Bobby, Jr., and Adam grew up at the tracks together and were best friends.

Hamilton absolutely declined to discuss Adam's death. Bobby Jr. told me he had "never seen my dad take anything so hard in all my life. When Adam got killed, it was like we had lost a member of our own family. It really shook up my dad."

Hamilton was so distraught by Adam's death that he sat Little Bobby down and tried to talk him out of racing.

"He didn't come right out and say, 'Please don't race no more,' but I knew that's what he was getting at," said Bobby Jr., a full-time driver in the NASCAR Busch Series. "He said something like, 'Look, I know how much racing means to you, but I don't want you to think that you have to do it. If you want to do something else for a living, I'll support you completely.'"

Little Bobby continued: "I told my dad that I appreciated his concern, and that I was hurt by Adam's death just like he was. But there was no way I was going to quit racing. My dad races, my grandfather raced, my great-grandfather raced. And, by God, I'm going to race, too."

***

Just as Bobby Sr. wrestled with an uneasy relationship with his father, so did Bobby Jr. with his.

When Little Bobby was struggling to get his racing career off the ground, his father seemed to take a sink-or-swim attitude. The senior Hamilton pretty much left his son to fend for himself, and at one point Bobby Jr. moved away from home and settled in North Carolina to seek his fortune on his own.

"For a long time I didn't understand why my dad didn't do more to help me," Little Bobby would later confide. "He was a big-name driver with a lot of contacts in the sport, but he wouldn't go out of his way to help open doors for me. Now I know what he was doing—he wanted me to get out on my own and learn. I realize now that he was always there for me, ready to catch me if I fell. But I didn't know that at the time and yeah, it hurt a little."

"The men in our family have never made a big show of emotions," Beverly Hamilton said. "My daddy didn't, Bud didn't, and Bobby doesn't. They've always been the strong, silent type. They keep their feelings inside."

"I know my dad loves me," Little Bobby said. "He may not say it; he's not big on hugging and carrying on like that. But I know he loves me, and that's all that matters."

Just as Little Bobby has reconciled with his father, so did Bobby Sr. and his father Bud, at least to an extent.

"My dad was a big Richard Petty fan, and he was really proud when I drove for Richard," Hamilton recalled. "He went to some of my races and was at Phoenix when I won my first one. I was glad he got to see it. It meant a lot to me."

Bud Hamilton died not too long afterwards. All the lost years with his son died with him.

***

While his own son was off in the Carolinas trying to build a career on his own, Bobby Hamilton took a special interest in a young Nashville driver named Casey Atwood. Atwood was 15 and racing at Highland Rim Speedway when he caught Hamilton's eye.

"I liked Casey right away," Hamilton said. "You could tell that he was a really bright kid, and he was really into racing. He wasn't just out there playing around. I started talking to him, got to know him and his dad, Terry, pretty good, and I told them I'd help them out all I could."

"Bobby was the one man who most helped me get my foot in the door," Atwood said. "I don't come from a racing background; nobody in my family has ever raced. I didn't have any connections in the sport, nobody with experience who I could turn to for advice. That is, until Bobby came along. He was my 'racing insider' and he really helped me out."

"I remember when Darrell Waltrip did the same thing for me," Hamilton said. "He was an established driver who knew what he was doing and took the time to work with me, introduce me around, show me the ropes. He didn't have to, but he did, and I probably wouldn't have made it in racing if it hadn't been for him. I'll always appreciate it.

"Hopefully I was able to help Casey some, the way Darrell once helped me."

***

Unlike most star drivers, I get the feeling that Bobby Hamilton is not totally consumed by the sport.

As I said earlier, he has never craved publicity and attention. I think he enjoys the competition, tinkering with the cars, but mostly he views driving a race car much the same way he viewed driving a wrecker—a way to make a living.

Hamilton walked away from Winston Cup racing after the end of the 2002 season. He expressed no regrets. He said he intends to devote his time to overseeing his NASCAR Craftsman Truck Series teams. He fields three trucks and plans to drive one of them himself.

Talk about a career coming full-circle: Hamilton began as a truck driver and will end as a truck driver. Of course the difference is that the trucks he plans to drive in the future don't have hooks on the back, and he won't be towing away cars with them. No angry owners will chase him down the dark streets, threatening to tie a knot in his neck, like they did back in his days as a wrecker-driving repo man.

Bobby grins at the distant memories of those bygone wild midnight rides and shakes his head.

"Now THAT," he says, "was some damn excitin' drivin', lemme tell you!"

LAP X:

THE TAXI DRIVER

Benny Parsons was not Richard Petty. He wasn't rich and famous and didn't have a legendary father who helped open doors for him in the sport. Benny grew up dirt poor in the Carolinas. He raced for a while without much success, went broke, and moved to Detroit to drive a taxi.

I always liked Benny. He had raced at Nashville Speedway a few times, and I'd done some interviews with him. Most of the stories had a familiar angle: "Hard-luck young racer tries to make a career in NASCAR."

Often when a driver falls on hard times, when his career is on the rocks, he avoids the media. Not Benny. He was always accommodating, even during his darkest hours. He returned my phone calls. He was patient and courteous. He was an underdog. I pulled for him.

Bill Donoho, who ran the speedway, also liked Benny, probably for the same reasons I liked Benny. Donoho had grown up poor, too.

A week or so before one of Nashville's Grand National races, Donoho called Parsons and invited him to come down for the race. Benny said he didn't have a car to race. Donoho said he'd find him a ride. Benny said he couldn't afford to travel to Nashville. Donoho said he'd send him some travel money. Benny said he couldn't afford a motel. Donoho told Benny he could stay at his house.

"To this day I don't know why Mr. Donoho took such an interest in me," Benny would say years later, after he became an established NASCAR star and one of the sport's most popular drivers. "I didn't have anything to offer him; I wasn't a big-name driver who could draw fans and sell tickets. I don't know ... all I know is that Mr. Donoho helped me out at a time when I was rock bottom. He gave me a boost that helped me get my career back on track."

Today Benny Parsons is a successful racing commentator for NBC.

"I've often looked back and wondered where I'd be today if Mr. Donoho hadn't made that phone call," Benny says. "I wonder..."

Bill Donoho died a few years ago. Benny Parsons was the only big-name driver who attended his funeral. Benny never forgets his friends.

***

One season in the early 1980s I was in Riverside California to cover the final NASCAR race of the season. Darrell Waltrip was in the hunt for the championship, and that was big news back in Nashville.

As I sped down the freeway early Sunday morning en route to Riverside Raceway, I noticed a car stalled on the shoulder up ahead. As I slowed down, I recognized Benny Parsons and a companion standing alongside the car, its hood up, steam hissing. I pulled over, backed up, and told them to hop in.

Benny Parsons enjoys a track-side cigar.

"You know it ain't gonna be a good day when you blow a motor on the way to the racetrack," Benny quipped, as he tossed a travel bag into the car. His companion, a lanky red-haired kid, climbed in the back seat.

"Woody, I'd like you to meet a friend of mine," Parsons said. "Bill Elliott from Georgia. Bill plans to race someday and he's hanging around with me, checking things out."

"Pleased to meetcha," said Elliott in a grits-curdling drawl.

Elliott would, indeed, go on to race. He would become one of the sport's top drivers and one of the all-time fan favorites. Apparently Benny taught him well.

LAP XI:

OFF TO DAYTONA WITH ROAD HOG

I strolled into the sports department one cold February afternoon, and the sports editor, John Bibb, glanced up from his desk.

"Why aren't you in Daytona?" Bibb asked.

"Where?"

"Daytona. The race is Sunday [this was Friday]. If you're gonna cover racing you've gotta cover the Daytona 500. You'd better get moving."

I quickly got on the phone. First I called the track's public relations office and asked if I could get a press pass. (Remember, this was back in the days when NASCAR was starved for coverage, just like the NFL. Then-NFL commissioner Pete Rozelle used to call newspaper sports editors and beg them to cover something called a Super Bowl.) I was told I'd have a Daytona 500 press pass waiting for me at the track's will-call window. The PR director also said he had some motel rooms reserved at Howard Johnson's near the track. He would put me down for one.

I was in.

The next call I made was to a former college buddy, Don Christopher—Road Hog. Christopher acquired his nickname from a hilarious impersonation he did of an old Statler Brothers routine, "Lester Moran and the Cadillac Cowboys." It was a parody of a live, small-town country music radio show, and Ol' Road Hog, with his gravely baritone drawl, was the emcee. Don could do a better Road Hog than Road Hog: "Hey, hey, hey! Hello to all you folks out thar in radio land! What purty number has Red and Wesley got picked out fer all you sick an' shut-in this mornin'? Honkey Tonk Angel? Now thar's a good 'un! Kick'er off, Wichita!"

I remembered how, back in our college days, Don liked to talk about racing. Everybody else was interested in football, basketball and baseball. Don's main interest was something called NASCAR. His idol was Richard Petty. Don talked about Petty with the same reverence with which the rest of us talked about Johnny Unitas.

I called Don's office, told him I was being shipped off to Daytona for the weekend, and needed a guide/technical advisor. I wondered if he'd like to come along? Would he? I thought Ol' Road Hog was going to wet his pants.

We pulled out of Nashville about midnight that night. Don had to make arrangements at the office. I had to draw some expense account cash and make sure the paper had a backup to handle the Vanderbilt basketball games for the next few days. (At the time I had the Vandy beat, along with racing, and wrote four general-interest columns a week.)

A long weekend in Florida in mid-February sounded pretty good. I picked Don up at his place and he tossed his luggage in the back seat, along with a heavy cooler.

"What's that?" I asked, nodding at the cooler.

"Man, have you got a lot to learn about racing," Road Hog grinned.

***

Along for the Ride 99

Richard Petty gnaws on a stogie.

That was over 30 years ago, and Road Hog has gone to every Daytona 500 with me since then. Tom and Huck never had so many adventures rafting down the Mississippi.

One night outside Valdosta, Georgia, Don reached down to change Jerry Lee Lewis tapes and accidentally knocked the car out of gear at around 80 mph. The engine screamed and shut off.

"Damn," said Don, "We've blowed."

Eventually we were able to get the car restarted. The engine had survived, but to this day Jerry Lee Lewis still makes me nervous.

During another trip the car's console somehow caught fire. Road Hog swatted at the flames with one hand, steered with one hand, and held his drink with one hand. (I know; it doesn't add up.)

I started to toss my drink on the fire, but Road Hog shouted that it might be flammable. (We don't do that any more; chalk it up to the creeping wisdom of age.)

Then there was the night we stopped in South Georgia for gas, and a seedy-looking strip bar happened to be located across the street. I let Road Hog talk me into dropping in for a few minutes.

As we were walking in, a couple of guys were walking out.

"Hey Woody!" boomed one. "What are YOU doing here?"

They were from Nashville, on their way to the race. They said they recognized me from my newspaper column mug shot. How embarrassing.

"Aw, hell, it could've been worse," Road Hog said. "It could'a been your preacher."

***

STP, Petty's famous longtime sponsor, used to host an annual Speed Weeks breakfast at the Indigo Bay Club near the track. It was a lavish affair, and hundreds of people attended—drivers, owners, media, sponsors, and race officials. It was *the* place to be.

During one of the breakfasts, NASCAR president Bill France Sr. gave the welcoming speech.

The venerable old patriarch introduced the featured guests at the head table, including Petty and several STP big-wigs, then with a twinkle in his eye, said that finally late in life he had figured out what STP stood for:

"Sex Takes Patience."

He brought down the house.

Launching an early morning at the STP breakfast had its hazards; complimentary Bloody Marys and screwdrivers flowed freely and profusely, and a lot of the media would not make it to the track until well after noon.

***

Next door to Howard Johnson's stood the infamous Boar's Head Lounge, the favorite watering hole for drivers and media during race week. Swarms of groupies were attracted to the Boar's Head by the rich and famous racers who hung out there. The Boar's Head was also called the Whore's Bed.

It was there, in the murky throes of one typically rambunctious evening, that the Legend of Rainbow Willie was born. More on that in a later chapter.

Another famous Daytona hangout, the Boot Hill Saloon, is located downtown. It's a rough, seedy biker bar, where trouble lurks in every dark nook and cranny. They have to turn the jukebox up extra loud in order for David Allen Coe to make himself heard over the steady crash and clatter of breaking beer bottles. The entire ceiling of the Boot Hill Saloon is decorated with women's undergarments. Road Hog and I have personally witnessed some of the decorating taking place. They keep the toilet paper roll chained to the bathroom wall at the Boot Hill Saloon. Road Hog says you know you're in a mean joint when the toilet paper is chained to the wall.

Major NASCAR policy was formulated many years ago in the murky, smoky confines of the Boot Hill Saloon.

Bob Latford and some cronies were sequestered at a booth, complaining about NASCAR's complex, screwy points system that was used to determine the Series champion. They began discussing a better way to do it—the media always thinks it knows a better way—and Latford began jotting down notes on a cocktail napkin: a certain number of points for winning, with a downward progression according to finish. He tossed in some bonus points for lap leaders as extra incentive. And a few more for leading the most laps.

Next day Latford ran the ideas past some NASCAR executives. The were impressed with what he had scribbled on his soggy napkin. They invited Latford to take a seat and tell them more.

Bob Latford, scribbling in a sticky booth at the Booth Hill Saloon, had devised the current Winston Cup points system.

***

One night many years ago Road Hog and I strayed into a country music hangout called The Barn, down on Daytona's main drag. We slipped into a booth and soon were joined by two gum-smacking young ladies with matching blonde beehive hairdos and knee-length white vinyl boots.

They giggled at our jokes, and one said she thought Don looked kinda like crooner Bobby Vinton—"You know, when the light hits you a certain way."

We ordered a round of drinks and gave the girls money for the jukebox. ("Play some Bobby Vinton," Don suggested.)

About the time the drinks arrived, one of the young ladies glanced up and squealed, "Oh look! It's David Pearson!"

Sure enough, Pearson himself had strolled in and sat down on a stool at the bar.

The two young Maidens of the Evening almost trampled Road Hog and me scrambling over us to get to Pearson—taking their drinks with them, naturally.

When we left, they were snuggled next to Pearson at the bar, gigging at *his* jokes.

They didn't even bother to wave bye to Bobby Vinton and me.

***

A couple of years ago Don and I—older and wiser—were in Daytona enjoying a quiet dinner at a seafood restaurant when Richard Petty strolled in, cowboy hat and all. A private party was in progress in a dining area in the back, and Petty was headed that way when he noticed us. He veered over.

"Why hiddie there, Woody," Petty said. "How's everything in Nashville?"

I said hello to Petty and told him I'd like him to meet a good friend of mine, Don Christopher, from back home. I said Don has been a life-long Richard Petty fan.

"Hiddie, Don," Petty said, shaking hands. "Glad to meetcha." Petty stood by our table for a couple of minutes, chatting.

"Well, reckon I'd better git on back there," he said, nodding toward the private dining area where a well-dressed crowd was milling. "Don't want to let the lobsters get cold. See you fellers around."

"I can die a happy man now," Don said, looking at the hand that had been shaken by Richard Petty, his boyhood idol. "My life is complete."

***

Daytona International Speedway is racing's version of Lambeau Field. Yankee Stadium. Churchill Downs. Augusta National.

It is more than a racetrack. It is a shrine, a Mecca. Mention Daytona and everybody, even if they're not remotely a race fan, immediately know what you're talking about.

A few years ago when Indianapolis Motor Speedway consented to hold an annual NASCAR race on its hallowed bricks, there was some concern among long-time stock car fans that the

Richard Petty tips his famous cowboy hat to the crowd.

Brickyard 400 might steal some of Daytona's thunder, that the mystique of Indy might dampen the aura of Daytona.

It hasn't happened. If anything, it has been the other way around. Don't misunderstand; the Indy 500 will always have a special place in our sports culture.

But dilute Daytona? Never.

***

"There is a special magic about the place," says Darrell Waltrip.

"It's almost mystical. I'll never forget the first time I drove through that big infield tunnel, came out the other end, and there it was: Daytona Speedway! I had to stop and sit there a minute and take it all in. A kid from Owensboro, Kentucky, had just rolled into Daytona. Man, I felt like I'd died and gone to the Promised Land!"

Other drivers recall experiencing similar reverent shivers.

"The first time you lay eyes on it you know you're looking at a special place," says Sterling Marlin.

"All those famous old drivers ... all the drivers you followed when you were growing up ... all the history. Daytona is the most famous place in the world for stock car racing. When you roll out on that track you feel like you're a part of history."

"It's pretty damn awesome," says Bobby Hamilton. "Every time I got to Daytona, I feel like I'm in church."

***

Daytona is not all glitter and glory.

The legendary old track has seen its share of sorrow and tragedy. Bodies have been shattered, lives have been lost. One of Daytona's darkest moments came in the 2001 season opener, when Dale Earnhardt was involved in a fatal crash on the final lap of the Daytona 500.

It's crunch time in a typically rugged NASCAR race.

It was almost midnight that night when I finished writing and filing the news stories, along with a personal column about Earnhardt's death—the single most publicized event in NASCAR history. Christopher was waiting up back at the motel.

Don had met Earnhardt a few times over the years while hanging out with me at races. Once, going to a party in a downtown Daytona hotel, Don and I rode up an elevator with Dale and Teresa. I introduced Don to Dale. Earnhardt grinned and told Don he'd better be careful about the company he was keeping; he said I'd get him in trouble.

"Tell me about it," Don said, grinning back. Don always liked Dale Earnhardt.

"Damn," he said softly when I got back to the room that night, "it sure is awful about ol' Dale, ain't it?"

Yes, I said, it sure is.

Not all trips to Daytona are fun.

LAP XII:

BRUISING BRISTOL

Bristol Raceway has always been big for its size. Bristol is like the pugnacious little bantam rooster at the end of bar, defensive about his diminutive stature, combative, ready to pick a fight just to prove how tough he is. That's Bristol. Small but tough. Cantankerous. Belligerent.

The track is barely a half-mile in distance, but its steep banks produce high speeds in close quarters. The field of cars stays bunched up, door to door, nose to tail. Kyle Petty once compared racing at Bristol to racing in a cereal bowl. Another driver said it's like getting caught in a cocktail blender.

The nature of the track guarantees a steady diet of contact and crashes, to the delight of the audience. Every year, Bristol's bruising races are voted the fans' favorite. Bristol has become one of the hottest tickets in sports. It holds around 160,000 and literally cannot build enough seats to keep up with the ticket demand.

It wasn't always like that.

Thirty years ago when I covered my first race at Bristol, you could drive over the morning of the race, stroll up to the ticket booth, and buy a pair on the front stretch. The track sat about 25,000 back then.

It may not have been a hard sell in those days, but it was a hard seat. The Bristol grandstands consisted of two concrete slabs on each side of the track. Hard, no-frills racing and equally hard, no-frills seating. That was Bristol.

Bristol was a tough track with tough racing, and in the early days it tended to attract a tough crowd.

The joke back then was that the reason why Bristol never had a fireworks display before or after its races, like many other tracks, was because the promoter was afraid of drawing return fire from the stands.

There were indeed shootings. And bloody brawls. And knifings—"cuttins" as knife fights were known back in the hills. ("Heard they had a cuttin' last night; some old boy got stuck like a hawg.")

If Bristol had been a person it would have had bad teeth, dirty fingernails, and mean, squinty little eyes. It would have had a raw, red scar across its broken nose, and part of its ear would have been sliced off in a bar fight. Its knuckles would have been scraped and skinned. It would have had whiskey on its breath. It would have been surly and looking for trouble. It would have been out on bail, or freed for the weekend on work release. Bristol was one rough customer back then. Still is, in a lot of ways.

***

In the late 1970s and early 1980s a friend of mine from Nashville, Gary Baker, owned and operated Bristol. Baker was a tax attorney for several Music City celebrities such as Johnny Cash and Waylon Jennings. Racing was a sideline. In addition to Bristol, Baker also operated the track at the Nashville Fairgrounds.

Baker graduated with honors from the Vanderbilt School of Law, one of the nation's premier academies. It seemed incongruous that a person with his culture and credentials would be interested in operating a rural racetrack that had a reputation as a haven for hillbillies and hooligans.

Baker didn't care what people thought. Despite his highbrow background he loved stock car racing. He even did some driving himself for a brief period. Waylon Jennings sponsored one of his cars.

Baker was a man of vision. When he looked at Bristol he didn't see a bullring full of brawlers. He saw the future.

"Woodrow," Gary used to say, "someday this place could become Daytona without the beach."

"Yeah, sure," I'd reply, keeping an eye out for signs of nearby gunplay.

Despite Baker's dedication to the sport, he was unable to devote the time and resources necessary to develop Bristol's potential. He eventually turned the track over to Larry Carrier, one of the track's original owners, who set about making some much-needed additions and improvements.

After getting the ball rolling, Carrier sold out to Bruton Smith, and under Smith's guidance and direction the place exploded.

Smith spared no expense in turning Bristol Speedway into one of the true jewels of NASCAR. He literally moved mountains, shaving down steep hills adjacent to the track and converting the leveled area into desperately needed parking lots.

Smith added several thousand seats, sold them out, and added several thousand more. He built a double-decker ring of gleaming luxury suites around the crown of the grandstands and sold them out as well.

Bruton Smith bought Bristol a new wardrobe. He shined its shoes, capped its teeth and combed its hair. He took away its guns and knives. He made the joint respectable.

But he didn't dare tamper with the racing. He left the actual track just as it was—cramped and ornery—and today racing at Bristol remains and wild and reckless as it was in its reckless youth.

Bristol is a time machine in which modern-day millionaire drivers peel off their civilized veneer and revert into a gang of crazed, brawling moonshine runners.

Dale Earnhardt once drop-kicked Terry Labonte out of the lead on the last lap. ("I just rattled his cage a little," Earnhardt sneered.)

Earnhardt slammed Sterling Marlin into the wall on the closing laps of a race, as Marlin was closing in on what would have been his first career victory.

A furious Rusty Wallace once threw a plastic water bottle at a smirking Earnhardt after a race.

Tony Stewart deliberately crashed into Jeff Gordon on pit road following a heated battle.

Kevin Harvick hurdled a car and attacked Greg Biffle.

"There's just something about this place," one driver once observed, "that makes everybody go completely nuts."

***

The lure of Bristol is not complicated: it offers non-stop action, tough, old-fashioned, no-frills stock car racing.

It's a driver's track. No fancy approach is necessary.

Strategy? Try keeping the fenders on and the car pointed forward.

Aerodynamics? Hell, Bristol can't spell aerodynamics.

Bristol, more than any other track, reflects the growing popularity of NASCAR as it overtakes all other professional sports.

For over 100 years, University of Tennessee football reigned supreme in the Volunteer State. Neyland Stadium expanded to 107,000 seats, and UT officials liked to boast that on golden autumn afternoons it was the state's fourth largest city. The City of Neyland, population 107,000.

But Bristol Speedway kept expanding, kept creeping closer to Neyland Stadium. Finally one day it pulled alongside, gave Neyland a friendly wave, and roared away into the distance.

Today Bristol seats 50,000 more fans than Neyland.

At one time the mere suggestion that UT football could ever be No. 2 in Tennessee would have been considered sports heresy; now Bristol annually draws the four largest sports crowds in the state: two Winston Cup and two Busch Series races. UT football has to settle for the fifth largest.

A few years ago when Bristol finally passed Neyland Stadium in seating capacity, I asked UT athletics director Doug Dickey for a comment. What has always been such a point of pride for UT was no more. UT football, for the first time in history, was No. 2 in Tennessee.

Dickey was gracious. "I congratulate Bristol on its success and its growth," he said. "The folks there have done a great job of marketing their sport and their racetrack."

A couple of years later, however, Dickey balked at an idea of Bruton Smith's to put a portable football field in the Bristol infield and match UT against a regular-season opponent.

Smith was convinced that such a game would draw the largest crowd in college football history. Smith even proposed an opponent for UT, Virginia Tech. I asked the Virginia Tech AD what he thought about the idea. He seemed all for it.

But when I called Dickey, he quickly dashed cold water on the proposal. Dickey flatly declined to go along with it. He expressed concerns about the complex logistics involved, about uprooting UT's season ticket holders who were comfortable with their Neyland Stadium locations. Luxury seat arrangements would be complicated to adjust, he said. Holders of prime seats might feel displaced; it could be a distraction for the coaches and players, etc.

I got the idea that Dickey's main concern what that the game might become a sideshow, a travesty, a gimmick just to set a world record. He had no intention of allowing mighty, hallowed UT football to be used in such a manner.

When Dickey declined to cooperate, Smith dropped the idea.

Smith said that UT, with its legions of fervent fans and strong East Tennessee ties, was the only team that could sell out such a track-and-field game. He said there were no hard feelings; it had been just an idea.

UT and Bristol Speedway have long shared a mutual fan base. Race fans flock to UT games, and Big Orange caps and T-shirts are a familiar part of the color scheme in Bristol's grandstands. UT sports information director Bud Ford is a long-time NASCAR fan who frequently attends races at Bristol. So do UT coaches John Chavis and Dan Brooks.

Chavis is a huge Sterling Marlin fan; he participates in many of Marlin's celebrity fund-raisers and often attends races as Marlin's pit-road guest.

The admiration is mutual; Marlin is a life-long UT fan who attends Vols games whenever his racing schedule permits. Sterling watches from the sidelines as Chavis's guest, while wife Paula sits in the topside suite with the coaches' wives.

Marlin once ran a special "UT car" in a Busch race at Bristol. Sterling and the UT marketing department collaborated to field a car with a bright orange UT paint scheme and UT logo and carrying a tribute to the Vols' freshly captured national championship.

When Marlin rolled onto the track in his Big Orange racer, the crowd went wild. A good ol' boy from Tennessee, driving a University of Tennessee racecar on Tennessee's only Winston Cup track. For the partisan Tennessee crowd, it didn't get any better than that.

***

For some reason, Bristol fans have always been especially tough on Jeff Gordon.

Gordon routinely receives fairly rough fan treatment at other tracks, but at Bristol his receptions seem extra harsh. At times it goes beyond booing; fans shout hurtful, hateful remarks at him. Personal slurs. Off-color names. Lurid epithets.

During the course of each Bristol race week, some media member invariably asks Gordon his response to such a hostile environment.

"They're just being fans," Gordon will answer. "I try not to take it personally. Yeah, I get a lot boos when I come to Bristol, but I get a lot of cheers, too."

The fans' intense dislike of Gordon could represent lingering vestiges of Bristol's bygone days, when it was rough and tough, rude and crude. Back then it was the opposite of everything that Gordon is now: suave and urbane, sophisticated, cool and mild-mannered.

Jeff Gordon is a tuxedo and Bristol—at least in the old days—a set of scuffed brogans. They just don't fit together.

Even today, with its towering grandstands and gleaming ultra-modern luxury suites, Bristol has not entirely shed its image of old. It still has a bit of the rawboned backwoods rascal in it. But at least there are fewer cuttins.

***

Lodging becomes a premium when the huge throngs of fans troop into Bristol twice a year. Hotel owners in Bristol and surrounding towns quickly surmised that during race week they would be able to charge any bloated, exorbitant price they wanted—and get it.

Hotels shamefully and ruthlessly gouge fans in every race town, and Bristol is no exception. A few years ago the city fathers announced that, out of their concern for race fans, they were cracking down on ticket scalpers. An ordinance was passed prohibiting the sale of a race ticket above face value.

Those same leaders, however, turned their heads when it comes to "hotel scalping." A scalper may not be able to sell a $40 ticket for $41 in Bristol, but a hotel clerk can rent a $40 room for $200 during race week.

The politicians certainly are looking out for the fans, aren't they?

***

Racing at Bristol had a profound effect on a young man who grew up in the town. His name: Mike Helton, who one day would rule NASCAR.

"I was actually born on the Virginia side of Bristol," Helton says. (The city straddles the Virginia/Tennessee state line and Main Street is the boundary.)

"I probably spent as much time on the Tennessee side as I did on the Virginia side. That's the way it is when you grow up in Bristol."

It was at Bristol Speedway that Helton first became intrigued with big-time stock car racing, where he began to follow the sport, where he first became involved in the media/marketing aspects when he worked with a local radio station. Helton worked his way up through the racing ranks, serving in administrative capacities at a number of tracks and, in the process, capturing the attention of NASCAR. NASCAR executives, including president Bill France, Jr., liked what they saw in Helton—hard-working, dedicated to the sport, an intelligent and capable administrator.

Helton eventually went to work for NASCAR, and his advancement continued. When France decided to relinquish many of his day-to-day duties due to declining health, he hand-picked Helton as his successor. For the first time in the sport's half-century history, NASCAR would be under the leadership of someone not named France.

Helton has proved to be an ideal choice, with his reputation for fairness, his popularity among drivers and the media. Under his leadership, NASCAR has continued to grow and prosper. Today Mike Helton is one of the most powerful, most influential figures in all of professional sports.

And it all began at Bristol.

LAP XIII:

FAST TIMES AT TALLADEGA

From the days of its birth in the late 1960s, "Talladega" didn't merely conjure images of the biggest, baddest, fastest, most intimidating racetrack in NASCAR; it meant party time for the circuit.

If you think the racing on a 2.6-mile track was wild, daring, and action-packed, you oughta see the infield. Women run free and liquor flows freer. It is *Animal House* on wheels.

Both the cars and the fans run fast, leaving inhibitions behind. Things go on in the infield at Talladega that would have gotten you kicked out of a Roman orgy.

Jim Freeman, former PR director at Talladega, is a long-time friend who got into racing after serving as sports information director at Middle Tennessee State University outside Nashville.

During one Saturday night prior to the Sunday race at Talladega, Freeman took several members of the media on a "fact-finding" ride through the infield. Before we departed, Freeman issued a warning: "Roll the windows up, and make sure the doors are all locked."

The crowd, realizing what was happening, was on its feet, cheering the Mystery Fireball.

Finally the cops threw up a roadblock in turn four. The pace car was forced to slow and then come to a stop. It was immediately smothered over by furious, embarrassed cops who proceeded to yank the driver out of the car like a dentist extracting a bad tooth. He was shackled and escorted away and would be given plenty of time to ponder his brief fling with celebrity.

He had led some of the most unusual laps ever run at Talladega.

***

Talladega hasn't been tamed all that much over the decades. Last year driver Tony Stewart called Talladega fans "the most obnoxious fans in racing." He subsequently said he meant no offense; he said he intended his remark as a compliment.

If by "obnoxious," he meant wild and crazy, Tony was right.

In the early years the area around the track was as untamed as the racetrack. Rural Alabama back then was no place for a man without a gun rack in the back of his truck.

My buddy Road Hog (you recall him from a previous chapter) and I once asked the desk clerk at our hotel if he could recommend an area nightspot where we might find a cold libation with which to wash the red dust from our throats after a long day at the track.

He suggested a beer joint in nearby Pell City and told us how to get there. We thanked him for the information, and as we walked away he called ominously, "You fellers be careful, now."

Good advice, it turned out.

We followed the clerk's directions, winding down a dark, narrow country road. We spotted the establishment up ahead, bathed in flashing blue lights. Three or four county sheriff's cars sat in the graveled parking lot, where the gendarmes wrestled with a shirtless patron, struggling to get him handcuffed.

It was as though we were getting ready for an
through Lion Country. Except that the lions are not
wild as what we witnessed that night: nudity, sex, exhib
drunkenness, brawls, mud wrestling ... a naked man
naked woman around a campfire; a buddy stumbled
INTO the campfire. One young lady did a striptease to
of a Hank Williams Jr. ballad.

A burly beer-gut leaned into a giant galvanized t
out another Bud, lost his balance, and toppled headlor
icy slush.

"Shit-far, somebody jump in and git Cletus before h
roared a companion. "And while you're in there get m

Fireworks popped in the sky, and the smell of wo
wafted and mingled with the sweet fragrance of burn
Woodstock had nothing on Talladega.

After a Saturday night at Talladega, the race is alr
terthought.

Race fans are a hardy lot, though, and the major
Saturday night and makes it to the track by race time

Once, one even had the energy to make history.
the pace car.

"We'd parked the pace car on the front stretch
prerace ceremony," Freeman recalled, "and all at once
down the track. I thought, 'What the hell's Elmo [P
pace car driver] doing?' Then I looked over and there s
looking puzzled as he watched the pace car disappear
first turn. Then it sank in: some crazy son of a bitch h
in the pace car!"

A tizzy of activity erupted. A fleet of motorcycle
into action, chasing the purloined pace car around th
driver refused to pull over. He made one lap, then
was starting to get the hang of it, dipping smoothly in
accelerating down the straightaways.

Track officials were scurrying everywhere; lawme
ing into patrol cars to join the chase. The driver st
stop. He swooped low through the corners, breeze
stretches.

Country music blared from inside, along with laughter and shouting and an occasional female shriek. The joint was jumping.

We crunched across the parking lot and stepped up on the front porch.

Over the sagging screen door a hand-lettered sign read: "Check Weapons Before Entering!"

As Road Hog and I had no weapons to check, we paused to debate whether this might be our kind of place. Suddenly, from inside the steamy, throbbing bowels of the beer joint came the crash of furniture, the sound of glass breaking, the thunder of oaths, and what sounded like the thud of heavy bodies being slammed against walls. A woman's scream rang out.

The sweating cops threw their handcuffed prisoner on the ground and, cussing under their breaths about "goddamn drunk rednecks," charged back inside for another roundup.

Road Hog and I drove to a truck stop, bought a six-pack, and went back to the hotel to watch TV.

***

A popular, semi-respectable eating and drinking establishment at Talladega was a roadhouse called "Franks." It was BYOB—bring your own bottle, then buy "setups" consisting of glasses, a bucket of crushed ice, and soft-drink mixers. Franks specialized in piles of steaming seafood and mountains of charbroiled steaks. It had a live band and a huge, well-worn dance floor.

During one late-night session, sports writer Steve Waid got up to dance with a cloth table napkin wrapped around his head, turban-wise. Another writer emulated Waid's headdress. Then another, and another. I think that even I may have participated.

That marked the official beginning of the "Brothers of the Towel."

Even today, when old-time sports writing brethren meet, one is sure to offer the greeting: "Brother of the Towel!"

Guess you had to be there.

My pal Joe Caldwell and I had dinner at Franks one night as the guests of Chip Williams, at the time NASCAR's PR director (Chip would survive the experience and go on to found a successful racing public relations company). That night Williams invited along his father and driver Alan Kulwicki.

Kulwicki was a quiet, unassuming young man, well educated, with a master's degree in engineering. He clearly was unaccustomed to such bawdy company and a boisterous environment. As the night wore on and heated up, the stories grew more ribald, the festivities more outlandish. At a nearby table a waitress threw a drink on a patron when he attempted to seize more than her attention.

Chip's father excused himself early. Kulwicki, perhaps out of a sense of politeness, stoically stayed to the end, quietly sipping ginger ale.

Next day, he told Williams: "Woody and Caldwell are the craziest guys I've ever seen."

We couldn't understand where he got such an idea. Maybe it was the napkins we wore on our heads.

***

There used to be a party in progress somewhere every night during Talladega race week.

The track pitched a huge tent party, with a live band and a giant barbecue pit heaped with thick pork chops and ribs. There were stacks of boiled corn on the cob and mounds of cole slaw.

Former racer Johnny Ray always hosted a cocktail dinner at his sprawling home. Giant broiled shrimp were heaped atop crushed ice in a galvanized washtub.

But nobody could throw a party like Boss Hogg.

Boss Hogg's real name is Richard Braden. He is a barrel-chested, mustached man, boisterous and full of life. Freeman gave him his "Boss Hogg" nickname after the sheriff character in the popular TV series *Dukes of Hazzard*.

Every year during Talladega race week, Richard and wife Carol would invite friends from the media and other hangers-on to a pool party at their home. I can only assume they had a good insurance policy.

The highlight of the evening at Boss Hogg's party was hitting the swimming pool. Everybody went in, in various stages of dress and undress. Or at least they were supposed to. One night Connor Gilbert, a writer from Chattanooga, begged off. He said he was too tired, the water was too cold. He said he wasn't going in.

Several cronies promptly yanked Connor off the deck chair on which he was reclining and began dragging him toward the pool, ignoring his pleadings. Finally, as he teetered on the brink of the pool, Connor relented.

"OK, OK," he growled. "I'll go in the damn pool. Let me take off my shoes and sports coat."

We waited patiently while Connor shucked off his jacket, pulled off his shoes and carefully laid them aside. He removed his wallet and placed it on top of the pile. He took a deep breath and jumped in. When he bobbed up, his coat, shoes and wallet were floating on the surface.

He should have gone quietly.

***

There weren't any five-star motels around Talladega back then. In fact, there weren't many motels at all. You had two primary choices of lodging: find a motel back in Birmingham, some 45 miles away, or accept one of the grimy little truck-stop motels near the track.

After a long night at Franks or one of Boss Hogg's pool parties, driving to Birmingham was not an appealing option. Most of us settled for the truck stop.

The motel wasn't that bad, if you didn't mind being kept awake all night by screeching air breaks, the grinding of gears, and the belching and growling of big diesel engines as the 18-wheelers pulled in and out, non-stop.

TALLADEGA 500 CHARGERS -- Three of
upcoming Talladega 500 NASCAR-FIA Winston
national Motor Speedway on Sunday, August
with his famous No. 71 Dodge, David Pears
Mercury and Buddy Baker with the No. 11

he hardest charging drivers in the
Cup Grand National at Alabama Inter-
, will be (left to right) Bobby Isaac
 in the No. 21 Wood Brothers' PurOlator
 Dodge. Race time is set for 1 p.m.

The smell of exhaust fumes and diesel fuel hung heavy in the dusty, muggy air. It seeped into your room, into your clothes, into your very pores.

You never forget the odor of a truck stop motel room: diesel fuel, mildewed carpet, stale beer, ammonia cleaner and some other odd smells best not to allow your imagination to dwell on.

Once, shortly after checking in, Caldwell dialed my room.

"Hey," he said, "I see they're using a new air freshener here—Old Dead Wino!"

Road Hog and I always roomed together. After one trip to Talladega he said he hated to complain about the accommodations, "but damn, Woody, that's the only motel I ever stayed at where they stole MY towels when I checked out!"

Hookers were known to work the roadside motels. It was not unusual to get a late-night call in your room from a husky-voiced Truck Stop Hussy wondering if you'd "like a little company."

Caldwell, after being awakened one night by such a call, asked the woman what she charged. She said $25.

"Tell you what," Caldwell growled, "I'll give you $50—not to call this room again!"

The working girls could be bold and brazen when hawking their wares.

One night, Caldwell stumbled over and opened the door only to find there in the flickering glow of the neon truck stop lights stood a young woman wearing nothing but high heels, a negligee and a smile.

He turned to his roommate as he sat up, half awake, in the other bed.

"Hey," he said, "Did you order a pizza?"

***

Talladega, of course, was not all fun and frolic, wild parties and zany characters. It was—and still is—a deadly serious racetrack. The speeds on NASCAR's biggest track are breathtaking—Bill Elliott was clocked at over 212 mph once. At such speeds the slightest swerve or bobble can spark calamity.

Not only have competitors perished on the track, there have been an inordinate number of unusual tragedies that did not involve drivers.

Nashville driver David Sisco lost his mother in an accident in the Talladega infield when she was struck by a truck while watching her son race. A young couple died of monoxide poisoning in their infield tent. A crewman was killed when a compressed air tank exploded. Another pit crewman caught fire when he accidentally sloshed racing fuel on himself during a pit stop. TV cameras captured the horrifying scene as he rolled and thrashed, engulfed in a roaring orange fireball.

Talladega tragedies became so commonplace that it was not a question of *if* something bad would happen, but rather *when*. That grim history inspired the birth of a legend: the track was cursed. Talladega Superspeedway was said to have been built on an ancient Indian burial site, and the spirits were angry over the raucous disturbance of the sacred grounds.

Call it curse or coincidence, something seemed to exact a cruel vengeance on Talladega's trespassers. Drivers sense a special nervousness about the place. Bobby Isaac quit during a race at Talladega when he claimed he heard a voice telling him to park his car.

Drivers perished on other tracks, of course, and crewmen and spectators have been injured in freak accidents at all other racing venues. In truth, Talladega's safety record probably is no worse or no better than other sites on the circuit.

But at Talladega, with its wide, yawning curves, its long, freeway-like backstretch, its sweeping front straightaway where cars stream through in a multicolored blur, everything seems magnified. The speeds, the wild parties, the tragedies. The good, the bad, the ugly.

There has always been a special recklessness surrounding Talladega—on and off the track.

LAP XIV:

DYNAMITE BOB AND OTHER LEGENDS

She's starting to show her age, sagging here, drooping there, looking a bit frayed and frazzled and down on her luck.

But there was a time when the old girl was the hottest thing in Nashville. She had a nationwide reputation for the fast company she kept, the wild weekends of which she was a part.

Now she's 45, and not even repeated facelifts and fresh applications of makeup can hide the wear and tear. All those long, wild Saturday nights have finally caught up with her.

I fear that Nashville Speedway's best years are behind her. Her bloom has faded. But oh, the stories she could tell—about the fast times and the famous drivers she once knew so intimately, the zany, colorful characters who used to flock around her.

I began covering races at the Speedway in the late 1960s, and I can attest that she was never dull. She kept things hopping every Saturday night.

A bit of background: Nashville has been hosting automobile racing ever since, well, since there were automobiles. Before they laid the first brick at Indianapolis, drivers were spinning their wheels in the Music City. There are historical accounts of "motor car competitions" as far back as the turn of the century. Legendary Barney Oldfield came to Nashville to race his famed Green Hornet on a harness-racing layout at the State Fairgrounds.

It was on that same site, many years later, that Nashville Speedway was built. Its gates swung open in 1958. The track, as was typical of many early-day racetracks, was part of the Fairgrounds facility. In the south, stock car races were as much a part of the State Fair as corn dogs and candied apples.

The track is owned and overseen by the city, which issues a contract to a promoter to operate the Speedway in exchange for a percentage of the profits. Bill Donoho was one of the first promoters, and it was under his watch that the track hooked up with NASCAR and gained national prominence. Donoho was a retired Nashville assistant police chief who got involved in racing for one reason, and only one: he looked at the track and saw dollar signs. Donoho was tough as nails, and he ran his racetrack with an iron fist. Did I mention that he packed a pistol?

I was in Donoho's Speedway office one night after a race when a driver came storming in. He had just left the payout window (in those days drivers were paid off in cash, immediately after the race), and he claimed he had been shortchanged on his prize money.

Donoho ordered him out of the office; he told the driver he had been paid exactly what he had coming.

"You're a damn liar!" snapped the driver.

In a flash, Donoho sprang across the room, hit the driver in the chest with his forearm, and slammed him against the wall.

"You son of a bitch, don't you ever call me a liar!" roared Donoho.

He grabbed the driver by the throat and began shaking him like a terrier shakes a rat. Donoho, at the time well into his 60s, was big and hulking and strong as a plow horse. The stunned driver, his face crimson and eyes bulging, struggled and gasped for breath. Finally he managed to wheeze an apology. He said maybe he had miscounted. Donoho loosened his grip and the driver quickly stumbled out the door.

I'd gone to cover a race and for a moment I thought I was going to end up writing about a murder.

***

The sport was wild and reckless and untamed back then. Promoters were known to play fast and loose with the purses—as well as with the rules—and heated confrontations like the one I witnessed were commonplace.

Meanwhile, down on the track, drivers tended to settle personal disputes with fists and tire irons.

Stock car racing had a reputation as an entertainment for ruffians, rowdies and roughnecks. And it was not entirely undeserved. Many a time I interviewed a driver who was oozing fresh blood from a postrace dispute and smelling like he had been using Jack Daniels for mouthwash.

A promoter had to be tough in order to ride herd over such a wild bunch, and Donoho, as you might have ascertained, was up to the task.

"Don't ever let those SOBs get the upper hand," he used to say. "You do, and the inmates will soon be running the asylum."

Donoho's showdowns with drivers were not limited to the Saturday night warriors, the local Good Ol' Boys who swaggered into town every weekend to raise a little hell on wheels. The Speedway also hosted two annual Grand National (now Winston Cup) races, and Donoho could be as ornery with the big-name drivers as he was with the regulars.

Donoho once became involved in a personal feud with Cale Yarborough—at the time one of the top drivers in NASCAR—over (what else?) money.

In those days it was not uncommon for a promoter to slip a star driver a little extra "appearance money" to encourage his, well, appearance. After one race, Yarborough claimed that Donoho reneged on the amount of money they had agreed on—I think the disputed difference was $50.

Understand, at this time, both Donoho and Yarborough probably were millionaires. But what's $50 among enemies? Both insisted it was a matter of principle, and neither would budge an inch.

After one of Yarborough's Grand National victories at Nashville, he refused to come up to the press box for the customary postrace interview, just to spite Donoho.

"If that dam' Donoho's up there, then I ain't going," Yarborough declared.

Finally, after two or three years of bickering, Donoho relented. His feud with Yarborough had become big news, and Donoho, ever the showman, made sure there was a newspaper photographer present when he presented Cale with a $50 bill.

The two mule-stubborn old combatants grudgingly shook hands. One witness said that during the presentation Donoho kept one hand on his pistol and Yarborough kept one hand on his wallet.

***

Bill Donoho's son, Jimbo, had his father's knack for promotion and constantly dabbled in a variety of wacky ideas designed to draw a crowd. (In those days fans often came for the sideshow and stayed for the race.)

Jimbo brought in rock 'n' roll wild man Jerry Lee Lewis, who burned up a piano on the back of a flatbed truck parked on the track's front stretch.

Jimbo often cross-promoted country music acts. He got involved in a business venture with singer Webb Pierce that involved a Music Row swimming pool. When the two eventually had a well-publicized falling-out, Jimbo dumped a truckload of live catfish into the pool.

Naturally, he called the press first.

Jimbo loved daredevils and stunt drivers. He signed someone named "Dynamite Bob" for a prerace performance. Dynamite Bob's act consisted of blowing himself up in a coffin filled with flour for dramatic effect.

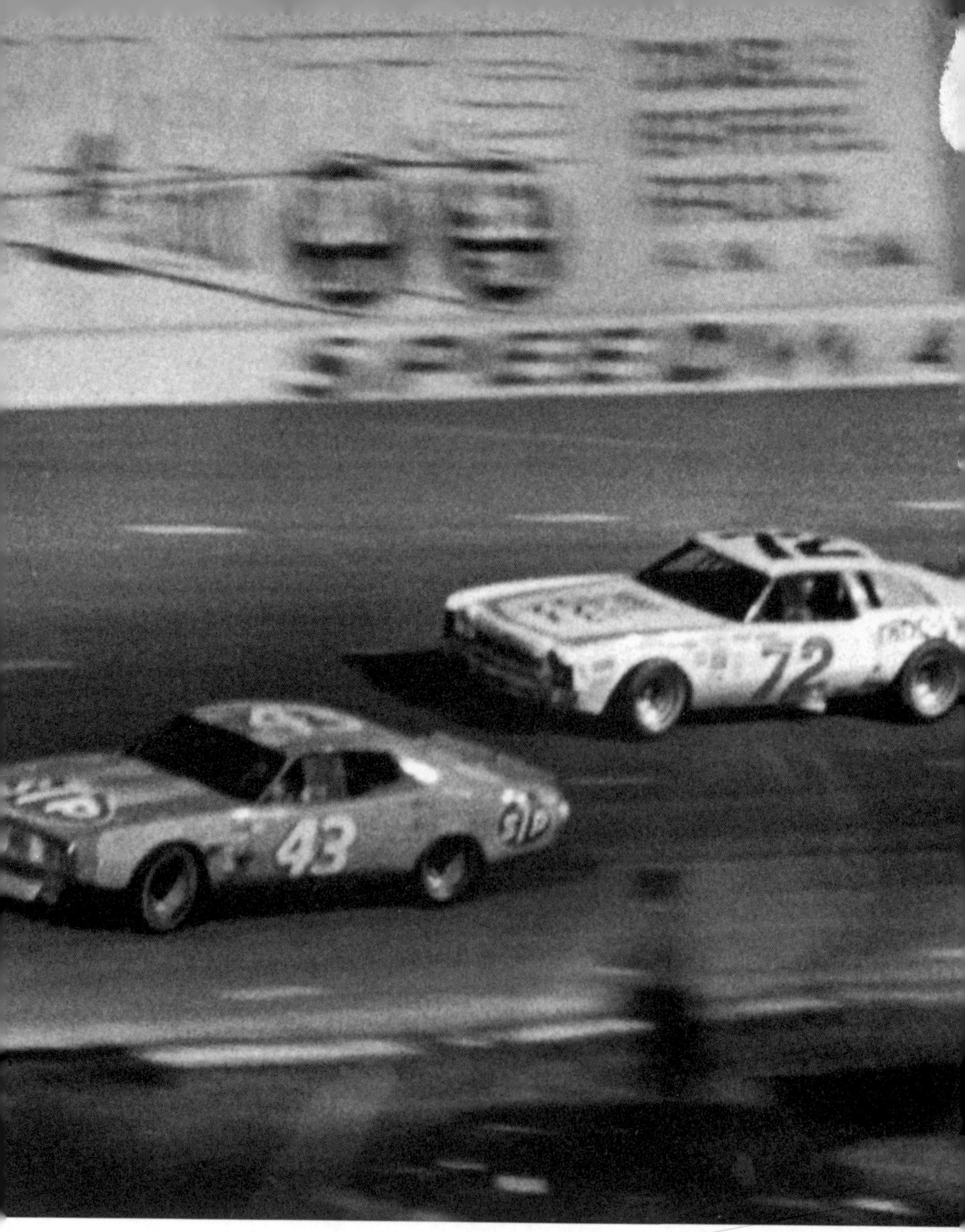
43
72

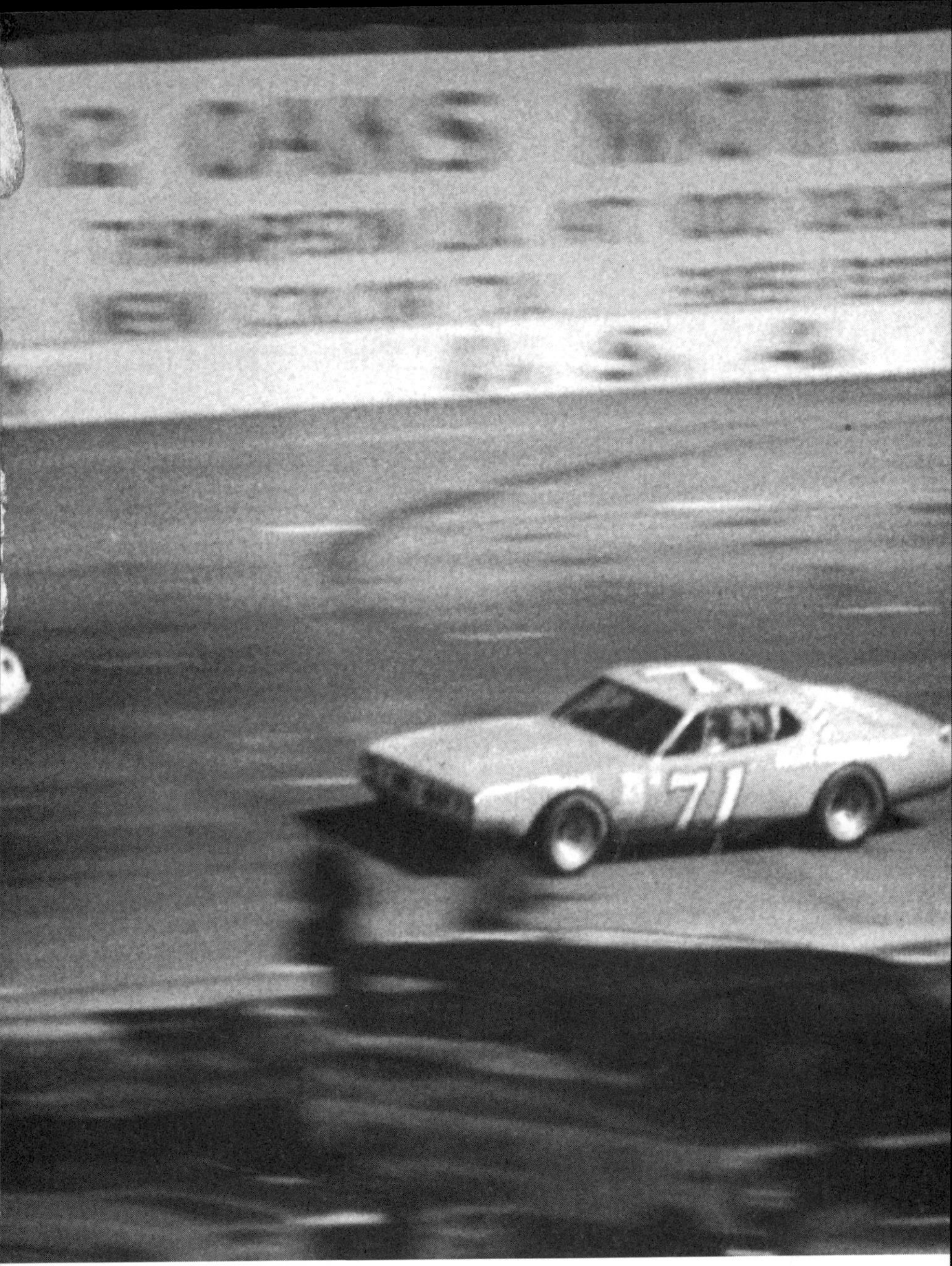

Dynamite Bob's connection with racing was always a bit fuzzy, as was Dynamite Bob after a few performances.

The Joey Chitwood Thrill Show was one of Jimbo's favorites. Chitwood specialized in a variety of driving stunts, including racing around the track in a car tipped up on two wheels. One night Joe Caldwell of *The Nashville Banner* was in the broadcast booth, teasing PA announcer Ed Hamilton about getting tongue-twisted. Caldwell succeeded in rattling Hamilton, who boomed into his microphone:

"And now, ladies and gentlemen, it's time for the world-famous Joey Thrillwood Shit Show!"

Another great moment in broadcasting: Joe Williams was getting ready to call the start of a race one evening when several puppies, disturbed by the noise, came spilling out from their den in a back-stretch culvert. The puppies waddled onto the track and the field of cars, still under caution, went serving and darting to miss them as the flagman frantically waved the yellow flag.

Up in the broadcast booth Williams calmly intoned over the PA system: "Looks like caution's out for a litter on the track."

***

An out-of-town driver came in one Saturday night for a race. Let's call him Bubba.

What local fans didn't know was that Bubba had lost his left leg in an accident and was equipped with prosthesis—an artificial leg. Bubba raced with the artificial leg, pulling his racing uniform on over it and wearing a racing shoe on his artificial foot.

Bubba tended to list a tad to the left when he walked across the stage during prerace driver introductions, but nobody noticed; in those days, lots of drivers tended to list a bit from a prerace nip of amber courage.

The race was about halfway through when several cars piled up on the front straightaway, directly in front of the grandstands. Bubba was among them, and his car was badly damaged.

It looked serious. Rescue workers rushed to his aid, as the fans stood silent and anxious.

Then, from inside the car—movement! Bubba was wriggling around. He was OK.

He slowly raised his window net and a relieved cheer began to build in the crowd—only to turn into a gasp of horror when Bubba tossed his leg out the window! Don't look, Edna—Bubba's coming out in pieces!

***

Nashville Speedway was a favorite hangout for country music stars. In the South, country music and stock car racing go together like grits and butter. Jimbo Donoho once produced an album titled "NASCAR Goes Country." It featured songs by Richard Petty, Bobby Allison, David Pearson, Darrell Waltrip and Cale Yarborough.

How did it do? Let's just say that it didn't exactly bump Merle Haggard off the charts.

Famed country crooner Marty Robbins wrote a song about racing. Marty didn't just sing about it, he lived it. Marty loved the speed, the challenge, and the thrill.

Every Saturday night when he wasn't on the road, Marty could be found at the Fairgrounds. He always requested the final set on the Grand Ole Opry in order to allow him more time to race. As soon as the race was over, Marty would rush downtown to the old Ryman Auditorium, where the rhinestone racer would stroll onto the stage still wearing the grime and sweat of the track.

Marty Robbins was a serious racer, not just at his hometown Nashville track, but also on such daunting ovals as Daytona and Talladega. He named his race cars "Devil Woman," after one of his hit songs.

Marty Robbins was a popular figure at Fairgrounds Speedway.

As much as he loved the sport, he eventually decided to hang up his helmet after a series of hard crashes. I asked Marty what prompted his decision.

"I got tired of being NASCAR's chief wall tester," he said.

***

Many of the greatest drivers from every NASCAR era raced at Nashville: Lee Petty, Buck Baker, Cotton Owens, Fireball Roberts, Rex White, the Flock brothers, Red Farmer, Richard Petty, Cale Yarborough, David Pearson, Bobby Allison, Donnie Allison, Davey Allison, Buddy Baker, Bill Elliott, Rusty Wallace, Dale Earnhardt, Neil Bonnett, Geoff Bodine, Ken Schrader, Ricky Rudd, Benny Parsons and, of course, hometown hero Darrell Waltrip.

The track helped launch the Winston Cup careers of Sterling Marlin, Bobby Hamilton, Jeff Green, Jeremy Mayfield, and Casey Atwood.

Then there were the local knights of the asphalt, drivers with colorful names like Bullet Bob (Reuther, who won the first track championship in 1958 and became godfather to Bobby Hamilton), Coo Coo (Marlin, Sterling's dad, who raced for a dozen years in NASCAR's big leagues), Flookie, Paddlefoot, Fat Boy and Smut (Means, another driver who went on to Winston Cup). Smut got his nickname because he was always dirty from working on his race cars.

Those were the days.

Time gradually caught up with the legendary old track. The biggest jolt came in 1984 when ongoing track management problems prompted NASCAR to terminate its two annual Winston Cup races. In the midst of the turmoil, with the future of big-time racing in Nashville dangling in the balance, I covered a meeting of the State Fair Board that oversees the facility.

The meeting was called to try to come up with some 11th-hour, last-ditch measure to perhaps save the races. Instead, it disintegrated into a squabble over who was responsible for patching

Darrell Waltrip and Buddy Baker chat with country music star Jeannie C. Riley during a trip to Nashville.

a leak in the office roof—the Fair Board or the track operator. With races worth hundreds of millions of dollars on the line, they were bickering over a bucket of roofing tar.

I left the meeting knowing that racing, as Nashville had known it for so many years, was over.

In truth, NASCAR's bailout was only a matter of time. The sport was starting to undergo a sonic-boom explosion in growth and popularity, and the little track had fallen behind. It couldn't or wouldn't modernize and keep up, and so, like the little rural track in North Wilkesboro, N.C., it got left behind. The old girl had grown too old and too tired to keep pace. But oh, what a fling she had back in her prime.

***

Even though the premier Winston Cup races were gone, a grizzled old promoter named Bob Harmon (Uncle Bob as he was known throughout racing) detected faint, lingering signs of life in the Nashville track. Harmon, who had been promoting races down in Alabama for the better part of a half-century, took control of the Speedway. He brought in NASCAR's second-tier Busch Series and rejuvenated the weekly program. Harmon, with his booming voice and P. T. Barnum flair, was the consummate promoter. Like Donoho decades before, he had a special knack for creating a spectacle, generating interest, rousing a crowd.

Darrell Waltrip recalled the first time he saw Harmon: "I was running a race at some little track down in Alabama, and things had been pretty low-key leading up to driver introductions. All of sudden this guy in a wild pink and white striped sports jacket jumped up on the stage and began to shout into a microphone. He started telling the crowd to keep an eye on old so-and-so, because he had vowed to take out some other so-and-so, and that there was going be BIG TROUBLE before it's over.

"He went on and on like that, and before long he had the fans stirred up. They were on their feet, booing the drivers, calling us names, hollering and carrying on. Harmon even got the drivers riled up. They started growling and muttering at each other up there on the stage. I was afraid he was going to get a fight started before the race even began.

"That was my introduction to Uncle Bob Harmon. Man, did he know how to create a commotion and fire up a crowd. I remember thinking to myself, 'Now THERE's a promoter!'"

***

Harmon's health began to decline, and eventually he turned operation of the track over to Dennis Grau. Harmon retired to his home in Prattville, Ala., where in the summer of 2002 he lost a battle with cancer. With Harmon's passing so passed a rich, colorful era in racing.

Harmon was perhaps the last of the old-time promoters, men who barked at the crowd through a microphone from the back of a flatbed truck, rousing the fans, whipping up excitement.

Some said that the sport had passed promoters like Harmon by, that they, like the old tracks, had outlived their usefulness. Racing had entered a new era—the fast-paced age of the Internet, space satellites, cell phones and fiber optics.

They said there's no place for a gravelly-voiced old promoter in a candy-striped jacket hawking stock car racing the way a carnival barker hustles a hootchie-cootchie show: "Hubba, hubba, hubba! Right this way, folks! Get your tickets! Wheweeeeee, have we got a show for you!"

Maybe they're right. Maybe it's time for a new generation, with new ideas.

The show will go on without the Uncle Bobs of the sport. But it sure doesn't seem to be as much fun any more.

LAP XV:

BITS AND PIECES

I never knew Junior Johnson that well, but what I did know about him, I admired. I never saw Junior drive a race car, but I covered his years as a team owner, during which time Nashville-area drivers Darrell Waltrip and Sterling Marlin served stints with him. Junior was already a legend by that time, immortalized by author Tom Wolf as the *Last American Hero*. He was a tough racer in his day, rising from a hardscrabble upbringing as the son of a moonshiner—and proud of it.

Junior ran 'shine too. He was never caught by the government revenuers on the road, but they finally nabbed him in an ambush. They staked out his daddy's still and caught Junior one early dawn when he showed up to tend it. He was sentenced to a short stint in prison and served his time quietly.

I thought Junior had a good perspective on the moonshining profession. He pointed out that the government wasn't opposed to making liquor, selling liquor, or drinking liquor.

The only thing the Feds were opposed to was not getting their cut off the top. Since moonshiners paid no tax on their product, the Feds were determined to shut them down. Moonshine raids weren't about morality; they were about money.

A lot of mountain folk back then considered moonshining an honorable profession. It was hard, backbreaking work, hauling the ingredients into the rugged hills where the stills were hidden, tending the stills, then hauling out the finished product.

As Junior once said, the options weren't all that varied for poor folk back in his area: run moonshine or go on welfare—choose the latter and you could sit back and let the government support you; opt for the former, and the government would try to hunt you down.

The most dangerous part of moonshining was in the delivery, making the runs to distribute the illegal cargos of "mountain dew." The money was good but the risks were great. The Feds were serious.

Frankly, I suspect a lot of moonshine runners were drawn to the trade not just by the money, but also by the thrill. They enjoyed the high-speed, "Thunder Road" chases, the game of wits with the revenuers, the daring and the danger.

They were reckless daredevils, those moonshine runners. They were the original stock car racers.

***

Junior Johnson ran his first race in what he called a "liquor car," a souped-up car used to haul moonshine. It belonged to his brother. The story of Junior's first ride is a slice of pure mountain Americana.

Here's how Junior tells it: "I was out plowing one day, walking along barefoot behind an old mule, when my brother drove up in his liquor car. There was a race going on somewhere that afternoon, and for whatever reason my brother couldn't make it. He wanted to know if I'd race the car for him. I told him to wait a minute, while I tied up the mule and put on my shoes."

A racing legend was born.

In those days, moonshine runners liked to boast about who had the fastest cars. They began holding showdowns in cow pastures, racing against each other. Side bets would be made. Gradually word got out about the moonshine runners' duels, and spectators started showing up to watch the spectacle.

Before long someone had an idea: set up a few benches for the spectators to sit on and charge admission.

The sport of stock car racing was off and running.

Junior Johnson's contribution to the sport consists of much more than just providing some colorful early chapters in the history book. It was Johnson who introduced R. J. Reynolds Tobacco to NASCAR, and the arrangement pumped mega-millions of dollars into the sport over the years. It signaled the beginning of major corporate sponsorships that today are the life's blood of racing.

It is an impressive legacy for a barefoot mountain boy.

***

They called him Handsome Harry Gant. There was never a cooler racer in NASCAR.

My most enduring impression of Gant: he came to Nashville one Saturday night to run a Sportsman race that had attracted most of the big names in the regional series from the South and Southeast: Butch Lindley, L. D. Ottinger, Jack Ingram.

The racing was typically fast and furious, with fenders scraping and sparks flying. Suddenly Gant's car was spun sideways, where it was T-boned by a trailing racer. It crashed headlong into the wall, bounced back onto the track, and was nailed again by another car. It looked bad. Gant's car wasn't recognizable as a car any more; it was just a wad of crumpled sheet metal.

I was watching from the infield as amazingly, Gant slowly began to extract himself from the wreckage. He didn't have a scratch or a bruise. I hurried over, as Gant was assisting a wrecker driver who was trying to find a chunk of car intact enough onto which to fasten a hook.

Gant was calmly sipping a Coke in a Dixie cup that someone had handed him. I noticed that his hands were not shaking. He was as calm as if he had just shanked a golf shot out of bounds, rather than totaling a race car.

I asked Harry if he was OK. He just grinned. "Oh, yeah, I'm fine," he said, as though puzzled that I should bother to ask. "Looks like my race car is finished, though."

I've always been amazed at how cool racers are in the eye of the storm, so completely unruffled, unfazed and unaffected by their close brushes with disaster. None was more casual than Gant. Handsome Harry was one cool customer.

***

Gant encountered one of his most unusual racing experiences during a trip to Nashville one summer. He ran a Saturday night race, and rather than haul his car back home to Taylorsville, N.C., at such a late hour, he and the members of his crew spent the night in a local hotel.

Next morning when he arose, Gant looked out the window and his car was gone.

"The parking lot where we'd left the car was empty," Gant said. "My first thought was that one of the boys [on his pit crew] must have moved it for some reason. But they hadn't. Somebody had pulled up in the middle of the night, hitched up the trailer my car was on, and drove off with it. I didn't just lose my race car; I lost all of my tools, which were in a box on the trailer. It was about the biggest setback I've had in racing; I had to basically start all over. It took me a long time to recover from it."

Gant's pilfered race car was never found.

***

I met Rusty Wallace for the first time many years ago at Nashville Speedway.

Rusty was in the process of making a name for himself on the American Speed Association (ASA) circuit. He won an ASA race at Nashville that day, an event that was completed just before a cloudburst. Wallace stood under a dripping infield tent and conducted his postrace interview.

I was impressed by how cooperative he was. He had just completed a long, grueling race and fatigue showed on his face. Yet Wallace stood around (there were no chairs in the interview tent) and patiently answered every question from the little bedraggled knot of local media.

It would be easy to say that back in those days Wallace, who had yet to venture into NASCAR's big leagues, was cooperative because he knew he needed the press. But it has been my experience that Wallace continues to be one of the most open, accessible drivers even after achieving superstar status. A couple of years ago I was working a story about Darrell Waltrip's pending retirement. I was compiling various drivers' favorite Waltrip stories. Nobody was more willing and cooperative than Wallace.

He invited me into his hauler that was parked in the infield at Indianapolis Motor Speedway, and we sat and talked for a half-hour. Wallace provided me the best material of any driver.

He told about the time he crashed into Waltrip during The Winston All-Star race at Charlotte. The fans booed him relentlessly.

"Until then, Darrell had always been the villain in our sport," Wallace said with a grin. "That day, I made him into the victim, and I became the villain. I've always told Darrell that I was the one man most responsible for changing his image."

***

Ricky Rudd has always been a class act.

Like Wallace, Rudd was always accessible and cooperative even after he became a millionaire celebrity. I admire Rudd's willingness to confront controversy; some drivers welcome media attention when things are going well, then duck and run when faced with a negative situation. Not Rudd. He hangs around and faces the music.

Years ago Rudd was caught with an illegal contraption on his car, and NASCAR made a big fuss over it. I wandered out into the garage, and there in the back of his hauler sat Rudd. Two or three other writers headed his way. Instead of ducking back inside and slamming the door, Rudd sat on the steps and talked freely and openly about the incident. Yes, he said, it was embarrassing. Yes, he agreed with NASCAR that the infraction warranted punishment; he was willing to accept whatever the officials threw at him. Rudd wasn't defensive or belligerent. He didn't offer excuses or alibis or whine that NASCAR was treating him harshly or unfairly. He took the high road and earned a great deal of respect in doing so. That's always been Rudd's style.

***

Terry Labonte is one taciturn Texan. He is stingy with his words, as though he has been issued a certain allotment in life and intends to ration them sparingly.

I was writing a feature story about what race drivers do during a rare open date on the Winston Cup schedule. How to they spend their time? What to they do to relax when they get a break from the roar and rigors of the racetrack?

I approached Terry and posed the question: what did he intend to do during his break the upcoming weekend?

"Aw, I don't know," he said, scratching his chin. "I'll probably take my .22 and go down to the pond and shoot snakes."

Ah, the lifestyles of the rich and famous.

***

No driver has a more terrific sense of humor than Buddy Baker.

Every time I'm around him he has a new tale to tell. Actually, most of Buddy's tales have been told many times over the years, but each retelling is just as funny as it was the time before. Maybe it's Buddy's droll delivery.

My all-time favorite is his account of a crash he had at some little rural track one night.

He picks up the story: "I wasn't hurt, just dazed a little bit, but the track's medical people insisted on taking me to the hospital for a checkup. They strapped me on a gurney and loaded me into the back of an ambulance. When the ambulance lurched up the steep banking of the track toward the exit, the gurney rolled back and hit the ambulance door. The door flew open and the gurney bounced out, with me strapped to it.

"They hadn't stopped the race, just put it under yellow, and the field of cars was coming around just as I went rolling across the track. I managed to work one hand free and waved at them to slow down. The cars darted around me, and the gurney rolled off the track and into the muddy infield where it came a stop.

"One of the medical workers came running up and asked me if I was OK. I told him I would be, just soon as they untied me and let me off that damned gurney!"

I've heard Buddy tell the story many times over the years. He often concludes with: "I survived the wreck, but that dam' ambulance ride like to have killed me!"

During his driving days, Baker was a master of the superspeedways. He is a big man—Big Buddy Baker they called him. Maybe that's why he liked the big tracks. They fit him well.

After he retired as a driver, Baker became a TV racing commentator. A *Sports Illustrated* "media critic" poked fun of Buddy's drawling, syrupy Southern accent. The *Sports Illustrated* critic's column was called "Air and Space."

In response, I wrote a column defending Buddy. It was titled, "Everybody's Best Buddy."

I said—sincerely—that I thoroughly enjoyed Baker's down-home style and deep-South dialect. I admired the fact that he didn't try to put on fake airs and use pretentious accents just because he was on TV.

I said that "Air and Space" was a proper title for the magazine critic's column—because air and space is apparently what he has between his ears. Buddy sent me a thank-you note.

***

Another driver who possessed a zany sense of humor was the late Neil Bonnett.

He used to tell a story about waking up in a hospital room following a hard crash. He was suffering from amnesia. He didn't recognize either of the two worried young women in the room with him.

"As I listened to their conversation I began to figure out that one of them must be my wife and one must be my nurse," Bonnett said. "I just lay there hoping I was married to the good-looking one."

Dale Earnhardt told about the time he and Bonnett went deer hunting. It was a slow day. Nothing was stirring. They met back at the cabin later in the afternoon.

"Do any good?" Earnhardt asked.

"Got a couple of cows," Bonnett said.

"Sure enough, Bonnett had shot a couple of old range cows that were wandering around wild," Earnhardt recalled. "I asked him if he was going to have 'em mounted."

Neil decided to get into the catfish-farming business. He built some ponds, stocked them with catfish, poured in the feed, and waited for them to grow. The venture didn't work out as planned, however. Someone asked Neil what went wrong.

"I'd been told that raising catfish was just like raising cattle," Neil deadpanned. "Did you ever try to rope and brand a catfish?"

***

Dave Marcis was NASCAR's ultimate underdog.

When Marcis retired in 2001 he had gone some two decades without a win. But he never gave up; he kept plugging along, trying to survive on a shoestring budget as he competed against teams with blank checkbooks.

One January the annual Motorsports Media Tour made a stop at Marcis's shop in Avery's Creek, N.C. Previously we had visited posh, expansive, state-of-the art racing complexes belonging to Joe Gibbs, Rick Hendrick, Felix Sabates, Jack Roush, Roger Penske and Dale Earnhardt (the Garage Mahal, as writer Mike Owens dubbed Earnhardt's multimillion-dollar layout).

In contrast, Marcis's "racing complex" consisted of a cinderblock building out behind his house. It was packed with used motors and hand-me-down parts. Marcis even kept a barrel filled with old spark plugs.

"I never throw anything away," Marcis explained. "You never know when you might need it."

For years Marcis ran on high hopes and low budgets. The man who hoarded used spark plugs while other drivers were buying Lear jets and private yachts didn't have a prayer of winning, of course. But he kept trying, for as long as he could.

Surely there is space reserved in the Hall of Fame for the driver with the biggest heart in history.

***

Mark Martin is the greatest driver in NASCAR never to win a championship—or at least he hasn't as of this writing.

Martin has come close, frustratingly close, a number of times, but always the title has managed to flit away, forcing Mark to settle for somber second.

My favorite Mark Martin story is one he tells about the times his father used to put him behind the wheel of the family auto while they drove the back roads of rural Batesville, Arkansas.

"I was so little that my feet couldn't reach the brake and gas pedals," Mark recalled, "so my dad would sit me on his lap and let me steer while he mashed the gas. We'd go flying off down the road, me cranking the wheel and him pushing the gas, harder and harder. I'd yell at him to back off and slow down, and he'd just laugh. We'd just keep racing along, slinging around curves and darting over those little narrow bridges."

Mark smiles as he remembers those wild dashes on his dad's lap.

"I'd be scared to death, but I'd hang onto that wheel."

***

I walked into the dining area of a hotel in Johnson City early one morning the day before a race at Bristol and found it packed with racers and race fans. There wasn't a table available.

"Want to join me?"

I looked over, and there sat Alan Kulwicki, alone at a booth. I sat down, and we talked about the upcoming race over breakfast. There was not a lot of idle chitchat. I remember that Alan ate quickly, as if he were in a hurry to get to the track, even though there wasn't much going on that time of morning.

I was always struck by the single-minded seriousness of Kulwicki; he was the most analytical person I've ever known. He had a master's degree in engineering, and he approached every aspect of life and racing—owner and driver—as an obstacle to be dissected, an equation to be solved.

In all the times I was around Alan, I never heard him crack a joke. I never once saw him horsing around, pulling pranks like other drivers frequently do. He was always coolly professional.

One night at a bawdy roadhouse in Talladega called Franks, Kulwicki joined some friends and me for dinner. The evening was raucous, but Kulwicki never entered into the revelry. There was a quiet, reserved dignity about him. He seemed out of place and uncomfortable amid the boisterous atmosphere.

I was at home when I got a call from the office one night. Kulwicki had been killed in a plane crash en route to a race at

Bristol. The editor wanted me to come in and write a column about the defending NASCAR champion.

I wrote "The Quiet Warrior." That's how I remember Alan Kulwicki.

LAP XVI:

THE BIG WHEELS

If Eddie Gossage had, as a kid in college, been able to remember which side of the paper went into the copying machine first, today he might not be in charge of one of the world's largest sports facilities, Texas Motor Speedway.

Gossage, a Nashville native, was attending Middle Tennessee State University when he got a part-time job in the *Nashville Tennessean* sports department. Among his duties was handling incoming copy filed by writers out covering stories on the road.

He got fired because he kept screwing it up.

A bit of historical background on newspaper production is necessary in order to explain how poor Eddie got his fingers pinched in the grinding gears of technology.

Nowadays stories are typed on portable laptop computers. With the stroke of a key they are magically whisked back to the paper's computer terminals for editing and processing. But back in the late 1960s when I joined the sports department, the process had changed little since the turn of the century.

Stories were filed in one of two ways: transmitted by Western Union telegraph or dictated over the phone—the writer would simply read his story to a rewrite man back in the office who typed the dictated story on a manual typewriter. A copy boy would then rush the typed pages over to the composing room, where it would be set in lead type, inked and proofed, and readied for the press.

Both methods of filing were slow and cumbersome. Sending copy via Western Union was time-consuming; the stories had to be typed on a manual typewriter and then delivered to the nearest Western Union office with instructions for transmission to the newspaper. That process was virtually impossible for late-breaking, deadline stories.

The only option was dictation, and there were severe drawbacks to this method. Often the story would be dictated from a boisterous press box, amid the clatter of typewriters and other noise and confusion. Mistakes were understandably rampant.

Writer (dictating into the phone): "…and then Cooper pranced in for the touchdown …"

Dictation taker (in the office, the phone receiver cradled on his neck, furiously typing amid even more clacking of typewriters, rattling of wire service machines, screaming telephones, cursing editors and other assorted newsroom hubbub): "What's that? A hooker danced in a nightgown?"

True story: Boots Donnelly, a renowned Nashville-area football player, coach and now athletics director at MTSU, got his name from a newspaper typo a half-century ago.

His name was Butch Donnelly when, as a Little Leaguer one summer, he threw a no-hitter. His coach proudly called the accomplishment into the sports department. Bill Isom took the information and wrote the story.

Next morning Donnelly was identified as "Boots" instead of "Butch." Henceforth he has been known as Boots.

Even when the transmission was clear and ungarbled, the rewrite man often committed human errors—typos—in his haste to beat the deadline clock. That accounted for many of the mistakes that were common in newspapers those days: ("... with the final seconds melting away, Johnson sprinted to mid-court where he took a final desperation shit ...")

It was such problems that prompted newspaper production executives to seek a solution. There had to be a better way. An evolution in technology was launched, concluding eventually with the aforementioned laptop computers and interoffice editing terminals. Computers replaced typewriters and software replaced copy paper.

But the evolutionary process was not completed overnight. There were crude forerunners of the modern-day portable laptop (the Teleram) and still earlier, the infamous telecopier.

The telecopier was the precursor to the modern fax machine. A writer on the road carried a telecopier with him and set it up in the press box. He typed his story, then fed the pages into the telecopier, which was linked to a telephone, which transmitted the images (words) back to another telecopier at the newspaper.

It was not as simple as it sounds. The equipment was bulky and awkward, and the process had to be carefully coordinated with someone back in the office. Both machines had to be set on the same transmission speed, the phone receiver had to be properly fitted into the telecopier couplers, and the paper on which the copy was reproduced had to be inserted into the machine glossy side up. Any foul-up in any of the steps and the copy would not transmit.

It was especially important to remember to insert the paper correctly. If was inserted glossy side down, it wouldn't reproduce.

Or was it glossy side up? I could never keep it straight. Neither, fortunately, could Gossage.

One night the University of Tennessee beat writer, F. M. Williams, was filing a basketball story on deadline. Gossage was working the office telecopier. On the first try the telecopier was set on the wrong speed. The copy wouldn't transmit. Williams—famous for his explosive temper—was livid.

He tried again. Still no luck. And again. Nothing. Apparently the paper was being inserted incorrectly. F. M. raged and

Eddie sweated. The first edition came and went, as the harried Gossage unsuccessfully tried to get the machine to work.

Williams, who claimed that Gossage had botched other transmissions prior to that, was furious. Next day when he got back to town, he stormed into the sports editor's office and demanded that Gossage be fired. John Bibb, younger than Williams and at times intimidated by the tempestuous old veteran, acquiesced.

That afternoon when Gossage reported for work, Bibb called him into his office and gave him the bad news.

Eddie's newspaper career was over.

***

As it turned out, getting fired was the best thing to happen to Gossage, career-wise.

Desperate for another part-time job, he contacted Gary Baker, then president of Nashville Speedway. Gossage had been a longtime race fan, had become acquainted with Baker during his brief stint in the sports department, and thought Baker might have a job for him.

Baker did. He put Eddie to work in public relations and marketing, and Gossage did such a good job that eventually Baker moved him to Bristol to oversee the operation of Baker's track there.

At Bristol, Gossage quickly earned a reputation as one of the most capable administrators in racing. He was briefly lured away by Miller Brewing Company, where was put in charge of the corporation's million-dollar racing program. Among the drivers Gossage worked closely with was NASCAR star Bobby Allison.

But Gossage didn't like living in Milwaukee; he longed to get back down South.

He made the move, landing a job as PR director at Charlotte Motor Speedway in Charlotte, N.C.

Gossage found himself working alongside promotional genius Humpy Wheeler and innovative track owner Bruton Smith. When the three put their heads together, the sky was the limit.

There were no boundaries. No track in NASCAR did more to promote the sport than Charlotte Motor Speedway, with Gossage and Wheeler leading the way.

Gossage impressed Smith just as he had impressed Baker, with his work ethic, enthusiasm, innovative ideas and can-do attitude. When Smith decided to build his mammoth, state-of-the-art track in Texas, he assigned Gossage to oversee the project. Gossage moved to Fort Worth, guided the track's development and construction, and then stayed on as general manager.

The kid who had once been canned at the *The Tennessean* sports department was in charge of one of the largest, most lavish sports venues in the country (and third largest in the world, according to one of Eddie's typically grandiose press releases.)

The day Gossage was appointed to his lofty position, I phoned his office in Forth Worth. His secretary informed me that "Mr. Gossage" was busy at the moment. He was in a meeting with Texas governor George Bush, and after that had an appointment with Ross Perot, the word-renowned billionaire and prospective presidential candidate. Mr. Gossage was picking hot cotton.

I asked the secretary if I could leave a message.

Certainly, sir, she said.

"When Mr. Gossage gets finished with the governor, please tell him a friend of his in Nashville has a telecopier that's not working and wants to know if Mr. Gossage might know how to fix it."

The secretary said she didn't understand. What's a "telecopier?"

"Just give him the message," I said.

A few minutes later the phone rang. Eddie was roaring with laughter.

"Woody, you sorry ....! Telecopier? I hadn't thought about that telecopier in years! You don't ever forget, do you?"

We chatted awhile, talking over old times, laughing over old stories.

Eddie is a great guy, driven and hard-working. He deserves all the success that has come his way.

Before we hung up, Gossage asked me to relay a message to F. M. Williams, the sports editor, and anyone else at the sports department who might be interested. He said to tell them where they could insert their telecopiers.

Glossy side up, of course.

***

Mark Dyer, like Eddie Gossage, is a native Nashvillian who worked part-time at *The Tennessean* sports department while in college. Dyer attended the University of Tennessee, where he was an intern in the sports information department.

In the summers he worked at *The Tennessean*. Dyer planned to become a sports writer. For now, though, he was chained to the copy desk, editing stories, answering the phone, doing the million mundane tasks dumped in the laps of part-timers.

One of Dyer's most dreaded duties was taking bowling scores over the phone. He hated it.

"Hi, this is Pla-More Bowl. I've got tonight's scores." Fifteen minutes of typing mindless names and numbers. Then, before you have time to get the cramps worked out of your fingers, another call.

"Strike 'N' Spare. I've got the bowling scores."

There were a dozen lanes in Nashville. All 12 faithfully called in every night.

One night around one a.m., Dyer finished his shift of drudgery and headed home to Madison, 15 miles away in the suburbs. Dyer rode a motorcycle to work in those days. He was roaring down a dark side road, wide-open, and didn't see the Black Angus cow that had wandered away from a nearby farm.

A black cow standing on a black road on a black night is a lethal combination.

"I never saw her until I hit her," Dyer recalled. "One second I'm flying down the road about 70 miles an hour, the next second—splat! I hit something big and furry. I remember flying through the air and thinking, 'I'm not sure I want to do this the rest of my life,' and the next thing I remember is coming to in a ditch."

Dyer came to about dawn.

"I was lying in a ditch on one side of the road, moaning. The poor cow was lying in a ditch on the other side. She was moaning too. We lay there and moaned at each other until a farmer came along about dawn and found us. He called an ambulance for me. I don't know what happened to the cow."

Miraculously, nothing was broken, but Dyer was skinned from nose to toe. He looked like he had been gone over with a giant potato-peeler. He was swaddled in bandages for week. He said it was hard to hear the bowling scores being read to him through the gauze wrapped around his head.

That was Dyer's final summer in the sports department.

Upon graduation, Dyer got a job with Jefferson Pilot Sports, which produced Southeastern Conference football and basketball games on TV. He rose quickly in the ranks, but despite his success as a sports television executive, he decided to change course.

Dyer and some associates in Knoxville launched a new business venture: NASCAR Café. Dyer, a life-long race fan, would be in charge of the racing part of the business. Another partner had the capital; the third had the restaurant expertise.

They built a string of the NASCAR-themed restaurants, and eventually Dyer moved to Las Vegas to operate the NASCAR Café there.

A couple of years later Dyer made another career swerve. He joined NASCAR, in charge of its marketing and merchandising division. NASCAR merchandise is a multibillion-dollar industry. Only the NFL annually peddles more apparel and merchandise, and NASCAR is closing fast. (I kid Dyer: It's so big and successful that not even he can screw it up.)

Every team, every driver, is part of NASCAR Merchandising. Dyer is a big fish in a big pond, and he loves it. He attends races, pals around with the drivers, and hangs out with sportswriting pals. (Mark can get you a good deal on a T-shirt.)

It is a lofty perch, an impressive climb, for a kid who used to labor long nights on the sports copy desk.

The best thing about the job? No damn bowling scores, says Dyer. And no damn cows.

***

In addition to Eddie Gossage, Nashville Speedway was the training ground for a couple of other executives who would go on to great things in racing. Ed Clark went onto become president of Atlanta Motor Speedway, and Tom Roberts founded one of the sport's top PR companies.

Tom, who nowadays works almost exclusively with Rusty Wallace, was recently honored as the sport's top PR official.

Another of Roberts's notable clients was the late Alan Kulwicki who died in a plane crash en route to a race at Bristol several years ago. Tom was scheduled to be on that plane.

"I always flew with Alan to races, but for some reason I decided to drive to Bristol that weekend," Roberts said. "To this day I have no idea why I did it. I just decided at the last minute that that this time I would drive.

"I called Alan that afternoon and told him I was driving up, and that I'd meet him at the track the next morning. He said OK; he'd see me there. That night I got a call from one of the guys on the team telling me that the plane had crashed. There were no survivors. Alan and the other three people aboard were dead.

"It's eerie. Why, after all those flights with Alan, did I decide to skip this one? To this day I can't explain it. I guess there are some things that happen in life that we will never understand."

***

Jim Freeman grew up in Murfreesboro, the son of a preacher, but he spent more time at sports events than in church. He became sports information director at his MTSU alma mater, overseeing publicity for the school's football, basketball, baseball and other sports teams. But his heart remained in racing.

Freeman was a correspondent for Nashville's afternoon newspaper, *The Banner*, covering races at Smyrna Raceway among other assignments. One year a PR job opened up at Daytona. Freeman applied and, with a recommendation by highly respected *Banner* racing writer Joe Caldwell, landed the job.

After a stint at Daytona, Freeman was transferred to Talladega (owned and operated by the same corporation that owns Daytona). Eventually he moved on to direct the International Motorsports Hall of Fame in Talladega.

There's no way to confirm it, but it's a safe bet that Freeman holds the NASCAR record for jokes told. Hear a roar of laughter erupt in any press box, look over, and there'll be Freeman: "There was this one-legged nymphomaniac, who walked into a bar leading a pig on a leash and carrying a bucket of oatmeal ..."

Some of Freeman's material could make Dennis Miller blush.

During Jim's days at MTSU, basketball coach Jimmy Earle named him "Flake Freeman."

But as zany as Freeman could be, there has never been a more proficient, efficient PR director in any sport. If Freeman was good in college, he was great in NASCAR. He organized press parties and media functions, arranged innovative driver interview sessions, promoted driver/media golf tournaments. Nobody was better at coordinating sports media functions than Freeman.

Freeman always possessed the rare ability to do a job well while having fun doing it. If there was a drawback to working with Freeman, sometimes it was difficult to laugh and type at the same time. But somehow we managed.

Now Freeman has slowed the pace and seems content with the relatively low-key position of curator of the Motorsports Hall of Fame. I've told him that's a fitting place for him: resting among the other old relics of the sport.

Freeman in turn reminds me that the Hall of Fame has reserved a special place for my liver, which he claims has set a NASCAR record for endurance and survival.

It's tough to get the last barb with Flake Freeman.

LAP XVII:

SONS OF THE INTIMIDATOR

Imagine that Babe Ruth had three kids. And that all three played in the same baseball game one night. And all three hit home runs.

That's what happed one night at Nashville Speedway when three of Dale Earnhardt's kids competed in the same race. Three young drivers, bearing the name of perhaps the greatest stock car driver in history. All in the same race.

That's where the Ruth/Earnhardt analogy ends. None of the Earnhardt clan hit a home run that night. In fact, all three—Dale Jr., Kerry and Kelley—were taken out in a crash. None of them were injured, but Dale Jr. recalls an intense debate following their wipeout.

"None of us wanted to be the one to call our father and tell him we'd totaled three race cars," said Dale Jr., with a grin. "Finally we got Kelley to do it—we figured he might go easier on her."

Eventually Kelley stopped dabbling in racing and moved into the marketing end of the sport. She helps oversee the vast racing empire built by her late father. I once interviewed her during a visit to Nashville Speedway.

"I think driving is a lot of fun," she said. "But do it professionally? I don't think so. I'll leave that up to the guys."

Dale Jr. took to the sport heart and soul. Even with his famous name, which he admitted "helped open a lot of doors for me," the driver dubbed "Little E" paid his early dues. He ran many races at small tracks like Nashville's with little fanfare or publicity.

One night after a race Junior sat on the pit road wall, grimy and sweat-soaked. He had peeled the top of his racing uniform off and was wearing an old T-shirt emblazoned with the name of some obscure rock group.

I walked over and sat down beside him and we talked awhile about what it was like for a young driver to carry the name of arguably the most famous racer in the sport. Was it a curse or blessing?

"It can be a little of both, sometimes," Junior said.

"On one hand, it's an honor to be named after my father, and there's no question that it helps my career. I get a lot of attention, a lot of opportunities, that other drivers my age don't get.

"The downside, I guess, is that the expectations are so high … people seem to think that because my name is Dale Earnhardt Jr., I'm supposed to go out and drive like Dale Earnhardt Sr. Those kinds of expectations are unrealistic. I guess I worry sometimes that I may disappoint the fans, not live up to their expectations. I also worry that I may disappoint myself, and not meet my own expectations."

I don't think Junior has ever done either. He has worked hard to make himself a great racer. I'd say that, based on the amount of apparel worn by fans at races bearing Junior's No. 8 and Budweiser logos, he is the most popular driver in NASCAR.

Junior is the perfect bridge for the sport's generation gap. Older fans like him because he carries the name and legacy of his famous father; newer fans are drawn to him because of his edgy, MTV image and attitude. He is a rock 'n' roll racer, a stocker rocker. He enjoys loud music and late-night parties, and although some are critical of his rock-star lifestyle, Junior makes no apologies.

"I am who I am," Junior says. "I don't pretend to be nothing else."

That evening as we sat on the pit road wall talking, I told Junior about the first time I met his famous father. I was too busy to come out the track to talk to him that day, so Dale Earnhardt came to the sports department to be interviewed. Years later, The Intimidator would be the biggest name in racing, a giant in the sports world.

"Your dad doesn't make many office calls these days, does he?" I said.

"No sir, I guess he doesn't," said Little E, grinning.

***

When Dale Earnhardt died in a crash in the Daytona 500 in 2001, it was Dale Jr. to whom the media turned for comment, Dale Jr. who served as a spokesman for the family during the next torturous, tumultuous days. Dale Jr., not Kerry, Earnhardt's oldest son. It was as though Kerry were the Forgotten Earnhardt.

Some time afterwards I was talking with Kerry about an upcoming trip to Nashville Superspeedway, where he was scheduled to run a Busch Series race. I asked him if he felt neglected, overlooked, lost in the growing shadow of his kid brother.

"No, I don't," he said. "I understood why everybody wanted to talk to Dale Jr. when our father died. He was racing in Winston Cup, and that's where all the media attention is. He was in the race that day when our father was killed. It was only natural that he would be the one that would be out in front of the public like that.

"I didn't mind; in fact, I was glad it was like that. I'm not very good at that kind of stuff anyway. I was glad to stay in the background and let Dale Jr. deal with it."

That didn't mean that their father's death hurt Kerry any less. When I was arranging the interview, Kerry's wife, Rene, asked me not to dwell on it.

"It's just something he doesn't like to talk about," she explained. "Kerry was devastated by his dad's death. Nobody realizes how badly he was hurt, because he's so private and kept everything inside, to himself. But I can tell you, it devastated him."

"I loved my father," Kerry said. (I had explained to Rene that I had to ask him about it, as part of the interview). "I've never had anything affect me like his death did.

"I'm still not over it. I doubt that I ever will be."

***

Kerry Earnhardt is more like his famous father than Dale Jr., at least in speech, mannerisms, appearance and lifestyle. Junior, a carefree bachelor, enjoys the bright lights and parties. Kerry, like his father, married young and started a family.

Kerry has his father's piercing eyes, his bristling moustache. He inherited his father's North Carolina drawl (talking to him is almost eerie; it's like hearing his father's voice). He inherited his dad's love of the outdoors, of hunting and fishing. He once told me about his young son bagging his first buck, and how proud his grandfather would have been.

Kerry's early family obligations caused him to get a late start on his racing career. He had mouths to feed, jobs to hold down. Unlike Dale Jr., Kerry could not simply pick up and head to Nashville Speedway or other tracks around the South and Southeast, racing and hanging out at the track.

"There was never any question in my mind that I was going to race full-time someday," he said. "The only question was 'when?'"

Kerry eventually landed a ride in the NASCAR Busch Series with a high-profile team co-owned by retired NFL superstar Terry Bradshaw. Bradshaw's partner is Armando Fitz, a Nashville native who played football at Vanderbilt. Fitz married the daughter of flamboyant Charlotte businessman and racing executive Felix Sabates and before long found himself immersed in the sport.

Although Kerry's racing career has been slow in developing, especially compared to his younger brother's rocket ride to the top, Fitz has no doubt that someday he will be a success.

"Kerry is very determined," Fitz says. "He may not be as flashy as Dale Jr. and attract as much attention, but he is a dedicated, talented race driver. Things have never come easy for him; he's had to work hard, do a lot of digging. But he has never lost sight of his goal: to race on the same level that his father once raced. He will get there eventually. I have absolutely no doubt of that. Why?

"Because he's an Earnhardt, that's why."

LAP XVIII:

BUCKSHOT-SPRAYING CHEATERS

Cheating has always gone on in NASCAR. According to the history books, the first winner of the first race was disqualified for cheating.

Glenn Dunnaway of Gastonia, North Carolina, crossed the finish line first in NASCAR's inaugural Strictly Stock race but later was disqualified for having illegal "bootlegger springs" in his souped-up Ford. The springs were designed to distribute weight in the car, thereby improving handling when the driver slung a load of moonshine whiskey down a dark mountain road—or, in Glenn's case, screeched around a racetrack.

When I began covering racing some three decades ago I interviewed Bill Gazaway, at the time NASCAR's chief inspector, about cheating. I asked Gazaway how many drivers in oh, say, a field of 40, did he suspect of cheating.

"All of 'em," growled Gazaway.

Nobody enjoyed playing a game of cat-and-mouse with NASCAR's inspectors more than the late Smokey Yunick. A mechanical mastermind, Yunick was famous for playing slightly out of bounds with some of his technical innovations.

The most famous Smokey story involves a prerace inspection in which his car was suspected of having an illegal source of fuel. The car had been getting inordinately good gas mileage in recent races, and NASCAR sleuths were convinced that the car held more than the legal limit. But where was it hidden? The inspectors dismantled Smokey's fuel cell, fuel lines and anything else they thought could be a source of extra fuel. They could find nothing improper.

"Hope you're satisfied," sniffed an indigent Smokey as he tossed his dismantled fuel cell in the back of his car—and drove away.

Smokey in later years insisted the story was exaggerated. He said he barely had enough fuel to make it back to the garage.

The mouse may have won that one, but over the years NASCAR's cats—the inspectors—have tended to triumph. Or at least they claim they have. At every race, NASCAR inspectors exhibit a table piled high with confiscated parts that didn't meet inspection. They have the table sitting out in the garage, in plain view of all the competitors, to serve as a warning.

But how many illegal parts don't make it to the table? Ah, that's the mystery.

NASCAR once hired Gary Nelson to oversee its inspection process. When Nelson worked for a variety of Winston Cup teams he had a reputation similar to Smokey Yunick's—a mechanical whiz who could come up with a shortcut or two in the path through NASCAR's rulebook.

Nelson went from being the chasee to the chaser. NASCAR's idea was, of course, brilliant: who better to catch bank robbers than a former bank robber? He knows how they think.

***

Who cheats in NASCAR? Everybody. Even the great Richard Petty got caught once with an oversized engine. Petty was fined but allowed to keep the win. Some of his rivals claimed that such a blatant violation deserved a harsher penalty, and that the victory should not have counted toward his record 200th win. But it did.

He who is without sin, let him cast the first rulebook.

Darrell Waltrip got caught one summer at Daytona with some mechanical no-no in his car. When I went to interview Waltrip about it, he was still steaming. I made the mistake of using the term "cheating" when I asked him about the infraction.

"It ain't cheating!" snapped Waltrip. "Do they call it cheating in the football when a player gets called for holding? Or jumps offside? No, the guy just gets a penalty for a rule violation. You don't say a basketball player is 'cheating' when he gets called for a foul. He just broke a rule, and he gets penalized for it. That's the way it is in NASCAR."

So, I asked Waltrip, what, exactly, should I call what he got caught doing?

"Fudging," Waltrip said. "I was just fudging a little bit."

"Fudging" cost Mark Martin a Winston Cup championship one year. He was penalized several points by NASCAR for an engine violation, and those points ended up the difference in a close championship race with Dale Earnhardt.

To this day, Martin's team owner Jack Roush claims he got a raw deal. Roush continued to rail against NASCAR when Martin was assessed another points penalty in the 2002 season. The 25 points Martin lost due to an unapproved spring in his car loomed large down the stretch when he began to close in on points leader Tony Stewart. Stewart ended up winning the title by a bigger points margin than the 25 Martin had been penalized, but Roush still was muttering after the final race.

***

During one particularly dominant stretch by Jeff Gordon, Roush became convinced that Gordon's crew chief, Ray Evernham, was cheating. Roush believed the secret lay in the tires—that somehow Evernham was treating Gordon's tires with something that made them stick to the track better or wear longer or generally perform better. Roush complained so long and loud that finally NASCAR stepped in and confiscated a set of Gordon's racing tires. The tires were subjected to intense lab tests, checking compounds and all other elements. Nothing illegal or out of sorts could be detected.

When the announcement was made that Gordon's tires had passed every test, Evernham couldn't resist needling Roush.

"What's in our tires? Air, Jack, just air!" Evernham crowed.

Roush still is not convinced.

***

Years ago the fudge-gimmick de jour of many drivers was nitrous oxide, which they used to give their cars a little extra boost for a short period—say the last lap of the race.

NASCAR inspectors were instructed to check cars extra close for the hidden nitrous oxide containers, but they never found them all. In one race a driver crashed and the impact broke the nitrous oxide capsule he had hidden in his car. It gave off a shrill whistle. NASCAR officials were waiting back at the garage when the red-faced driver was towed in.

He had blown the whistle on himself.

Contraptions vary from the sublime to the ridiculous. Rube Goldberg would have been envious of some of them. Sterling Marlin had a record-breaking lap at Daytona disallowed one summer when inspectors discovered something under his hood that wasn't supposed to be there: a box of dry ice, through which the fuel flowed in a copper tube. The cooled fuel burned better, producing more horsepower.

I asked Marlin where the device came from.

"Beats me," shrugged Sterling. "I just drive the car."

I asked car owner Hoss Ellington how the device got under the hood.

"Beats me," shrugged Hoss. "I just own the car, I don't build it."

I gave up. I thought about trying to locate the mechanics that built the car, but I knew what their answer would be when asked were illegal contraption came from: "Beats me. Guess the Motor Fairy [the Tooth Fairy's cousin] flew in one night put it there."

During his dominating days at Nashville Speedway, some of Marlin's rivals claimed that he was not playing fair. They insisted that the reason why his car race so much faster than theirs was because Sterling's had some sort of illegal advantage.

"I don't know what he's doing, or how he's doing it, but that car is all cheated up," growled one rival driver who had grown weary of eating a steady diet of Marlin's monoxide every Saturday night.

There was a theory among several drivers that the track's inspectors turned a blind eye to Marlin's motors, aiding and abetting his cheating. They claimed that the track owner wanted Sterling to win because he had a lot of fans. The more he won, the more fans came out to cheer him on. Sterling's accuser theorized that Marlin victories were good for business, and that's why the track was protecting him.

I asked the track operator, Gary Baker, if that were true.

"No," Baker insisted, "Sterling gets the same treatment as every other driver."

Baker also denied that Marlin winning almost every Saturday night was good for business.

"Fans want to see competitive racing," Baker said. "They don't want to see the same driver run away with the show week after week. If anything, Sterling's being so dominant is bad for business. Eventually it takes away interest."

The bottom line, according to Baker: "We have never played favorites when it comes to enforcing the rules."

I asked Sterling if he had some secret weapon, some gimmick or gizmo that—while not perhaps technically illegal—was giving him a decided advantage over the rest of the field.

"Naaaa," he said. "I got a motor and four wheels, just like everybody else. That's about it."

But how does he make his motor and four wheels go so incredibly faster than everybody else's when, in theory, all motors and four wheels are supposed to be equal?

"Superior reading of the rule book," Sterling replied with a straight face.

***

The lighter a stock car is, the faster it goes. That's why NASCAR has strict weight requirements and carefully weighs each car before it goes onto the track to make sure it conforms. Drivers constantly figure ways to lighten their load during the race.

One driver was accused of having a "disposable" rear bumper, barely attached to his car. At the first bump, the bumper would fall off. After the driver lost two or three bumpers in as many races, NASCAR officials served a warning: bolt the thing on so that it stays, or else.

The bumper didn't fall off again.

Another way to shed weight was to put lead shot—buckshot—in the car's hollow quarter-panels to pass weigh-in, and then dump the lead during the course of the race. The driver could pull a string, which would open a plug and allow the shot to dribble out around the track.

Coo Coo Marlin once complained during one race that buckshot was flying everywhere. "It was like driving through a hail storm out there," Coo Coo said.

***

Nowadays the devices are more sophisticated and technical. One driver was caught with a hydraulic gizmo in his car that allowed him to shift rear-end weight once the race started. He said his team had installed it during a practice session and forgot to take it off. Yeah, sure.

The current hot item in the Cheater's Hall of Fame is a device so secret that NASCAR is not certain it even exists: the mythical traction-control device. It is reportedly a computer chip that can be installed in the car and used to control the traction of the car's wheels on the track. It takes the guesswork out of accelerating in and out of the turns.

Such a gimmick—if it exits—is considered a major no-no by NASCAR. Why all the fuss about such a device? There is a growing concern that stock car racing is getting entirely too advanced and non-stock, that the sport is losing its human element to encroaching technology.

A computer chip would be the last straw. When the cars start being driven by computers, the drivers might as well sit home in their easy chairs and "race" with remote controls. NASCAR wants daredevils, not nerds with joysticks.

NASCAR officials have warned that if a traction-control device exists, no driver had better be caught with one. They're serious, too. Really. They're not kidding this time.

Somewhere, Smokey Yunick is smiling.

***

Waltrip was always philosophical about fudging.

"There are a lot of gray areas in the rule book," he said. "You're always looking for an edge. That's the name of the game, to get a slight edge on the competition. Sometimes you go over the edge and you get caught. You look good if you get away with it, and you end up with egg on your face if you don't. It's a game that every driver has always played. It's just a part of racing."

Gazaway, apparently, was correct in his suspicions.

LAP XIX:

WOMEN, WENDELL AND WILLIE

Stock car racing has historically been a white man's game. Oh, there have been a few notable women drivers over the years, such as Louise Smith, now 86 and as feisty as ever, and latter-day Janet Guthrie, and a few blacks, namely Wendell Scott and Willie T. Ribbs. More on them later.

But by and large women and minorities have been excluded as drivers. There was a time, in fact, when women were barred from the pits and garage areas of most racetracks. Judy Allison recalls once having to climb a fence to gain entry to Victory Circle, where her husband Bobby was celebrating a win.

In fairness, there may have been a practical reason for keeping women out of the pits in the early days. The sport was rough-and-tumble, and brawls erupted over the slightest provocation, real or imagined. Just one word, wink, smirk or smile from one driver toward another driver's wife or lady friend could be the spark that ignited a powder keg.

Not helping the situation was the fact that liquor flowed freely in and around the tracks back then. Alcohol, flirtatious ladies and a jealous husband/boyfriend race driver could be a volatile combination. Racing promoters had their hands full trying to maintain peace and order; having femme fatales running loose in the pits could spell trouble they didn't need. So women were banned from the area.

That didn't keep them from driving, however. Smith and a handful of other women raced fairly regularly in the 1940s and 1950s. Louise, from Greenville, S.C., was the most successful. She won 38 races and in 1999 was inducted into the Motorsports Hall of Fame.

She said it was never easy being a gender-bending fender-bender.

"Back when I was driving, I fought," she recalls. "I had to battle. I mean straight-out fight. The men pulled everything on me, but they couldn't run me off. I was as stubborn as they were."

That was a half-century ago; times and attitudes have changed, now, right? Wrong.

Fast-forward to Nashville Speedway, summer of 2002. Deborah Renshaw, an attractive 25-year-old driver from Bowling Green, Ky., walks down pit road in her racing uniform, on her way to her car.

"Bitch," mutters one Good Ol' Boy propped on the pit road wall.

"Yeah," agrees a companion in a greasy T-shirt, grinning and adding,

"But don't that racin' suit fit her good? Ummmm, ummmmm, ummm!" A low wolf whistle follows Renshaw.

She keeps walking, eyes straight ahead, ignoring her hecklers.

***

Along for the Ride 173

Louise Smith was an early-day female racer and now a member of the Motorsports Hall of Fame.

Renshaw was not the first woman to compete in Nashville Speedway's premier Late Model division.

Kim Ritter, a Delta Airlines flight attendant, began racing in the Late Model series five years earlier. Ritter insisted she never had any problem with her male rivals. Well, one DID spit tobacco juice in the seat of her race car one night, but Ritter dismissed that as "just joking around."

"If you're going to race against the guys, you can't have a thin skin," she said.

The difference between Ritter and Renshaw was that Ritter was not competitive. She generally ran well back in the field and never, in any of her races, was she a contender to win. She presented no threat to the male drivers.

Renshaw was different. She had money behind her team, good cars, and a fiercely competitive attitude. After a quiet 2001 rookie season, Renshaw picked up the pace. She began passing cars, running up toward the front. She didn't win, but early in the season she put together a string of good finishes and became the first woman to lead the division standings in the track's 44-year history. Later on Renshaw made more Nashville racing history by becoming the first woman to win a pole in the top division.

As her success increased, so did her problems with the male drivers. I'm not sure that all the resentment was because Renshaw is female; she also happens to be attractive, charismatic, college-educated and has money. She receives a tremendous amount of media exposure and has a promising big-league racing future — all things most of the local male drivers don't have, and realize they probably will never have.

A lot of the male drivers, who felt they had paid years of dues and yet did not share Renshaw's prospects, were jealous. Renshaw's biggest critic throughout the 2002 season was Mark Day.

Day, a veteran driver from Clarksville, Tenn., admitted early on that he was not convinced that women belonged on a race track. He said he would never permit his own daughter to drive a race car. He said Renshaw had no racing talent. He called her "Wreck-shaw."

When asked directly if his problem with Renshaw was because she was female, Day replied: "No, my problem with her is that she is a bad driver."

But there have been plenty of "bad drivers" in the division over the years, drivers who clearly lacked the skill to compete. None were ever subjected to the treatment that Renshaw received.

The bickering between Day and Renshaw escalated. Renshaw possesses a fiery streak; instead of being intimidated, she told Day and her other critics to go to hell.

One weekend around midseason Day orchestrated an elaborate plot against Renshaw. He entered one of his backup cars in a race, driven by a friend who had never competed in the division. The friend was instructed to park the car shortly after the race started, thereby making sure he finished behind Renshaw. (Under the rules a driver can protest only the cars that finish ahead of him.) Renshaw finished fifth that night (behind Day), and her car was protested, along with the car of her teammate, Chevy White.

Track promoter Dennis Grau had got wind of the scheme prior to the race. Worried about what was about to happen, he called a NASCAR representative for instructions. Grau said the representative told him that the protest "was totally bogus" and advised him to disallow it.

But Dan Renshaw, Deborah's father, told Grau to go ahead and tear down the car; he said they had nothing to hide. However, the postrace inspection revealed a minor engine violation—not enough to have given Renshaw any advantage, but enough to be technically illegal. She was disqualified.

As Renshaw left, embarrassed and in tears, a number of male drivers and other hangers-on stood around grinning and joking.

"We got that cheatin' bitch," one snickered.

Day insisted he was not picking on Renshaw; he claimed he suspected her car was illegal—even though she had never won a race or even led a lap—and was "just trying to catch a cheater." Day pointed out that Renshaw's male teammate, White, was included in the protest.

Nobody bought that excuse—not the fans, not the general public, and most definitely not NASCAR president Mike Helton.

Helton was so incensed by the bullying that he called Renshaw personally and gave her his private cell phone number. He told her to call him if anyone ever tried to pull a stunt like that again. NASCAR also sent a representative to the Speedway to warn the drivers about any future shameful shenanigans. Grau quickly passed a rule prohibiting any future "fake entries" for the sole purpose of parking and filing a protest.

The story went nationwide, even worldwide. Renshaw received e-mails of support from as far away as Holland and England. CNN invited her to tell her story to Connie Chung. HBO called, requesting an interview.

Renshaw declined most media requests, for two reasons: she didn't want to be perceived as trying to use the incident as a publicity stunt, plus she feared that some of the media might try to use her experience to cast NASCAR in a bad light. (Nashville Speedway is a NASCAR-sanctioned track, and the drivers who plotted against Renshaw are NASCAR-licensed.)

Renshaw's goal since she was a little girl has been to race in NASCAR's top division, and she did not want to risk alienation by casting NASCAR in a bad light.

"NASCAR was totally supportive throughout the entire ordeal," she said. "What was done to me was in no way NASCAR's fault. Mr. Helton assured me that he was behind me 100 percent, and that if I ever needed him all I had to do was call his number."

Some of the male drivers rallied to Renshaw's defense. Roy Binkley, who did not participate in the plot, said he was ashamed and embarrassed. Joe Buford, a four-time track champion whose team contributed money to the Renshaw protest fee, later issued a public apology. Buford said what had been done to Renshaw was "shabby and shameful" and he regretted having not tried harder to stop the plot against her when he heard about it.

Not everybody, however, took Renshaw's side. Every time she returned to the track, she was subjected to hard stares, muttering, snickering. Snide, crude remarks followed her.

"It was a very threatening, intimidating atmosphere," she said.

Grau said he increased track security around Renshaw; if he did, I never saw it. Even after NASCAR's warning she continued to be openly harassed and intimidated. Finally, at the behest of her worried parents, she quit.

"If somebody is low enough to do what they did to Deborah the first time, who knows what they might do her next," Dan Renshaw said.

"I don't think it's safe for her to be on the track with people like that. I'm afraid for her safety."

There was definitely a deranged, possibly dangerous element involved. Not drivers, perhaps, but certainly persons close to them and their teams. I began to receive threatening e-mails and phone calls at the sports department. Then at home.

"We know where you live," growled a nasal voice in the middle of the night. "We're gonna get you."

Some of the most vile, vicious and obscene calls were from women.

One day a package arrived addressed to me at the newspaper. Inside was a frilly bra and lace panties, along with a scrawled note: "Dear Larry, just a little something to remember me by, after all the things you've done for me! Love, Debra." They had misspelled "Deborah."

Dan Renshaw was right; there are some dangerous kooks out there.

All that—the harassment, the scheming, the intimidation, the threats—just because a woman wanted to drive a race car.

***

When Lyn St. James heard about Renshaw's ordeal, she was incensed.

"It makes my blood boil," said St. James, who was forced to fight similar sexist battles during her days as an Indy racer. "It's shameful. It's ludicrous. But I have to admit I'm not shocked."

Janet Guthrie, who became the first woman to qualify for the Daytona 500 during a brief NASCAR stint in the 1980s, echoed those sentiments.

"It is astonishing to me, absolutely astonishing," Guthrie said.

Eighty-five-year-old Louise Smith had this advice for Renshaw: don't let 'em run you off.

"If that girl gives up now, she might as well forget it," Smith said. "If she wants this type of work, she has to stay out and battle it out."

Renshaw is trying. She competed in several ARCA races in 2002 and was planning to make her Busch Series debut when a tragedy at Lowe's Motor Speedway near Charlotte ended her season. She was involved in a crash during an ARCA practice that took the life of driver Eric Martin and sent her to the hospital with a shattered foot, concussion and other injuries.

Renshaw spent the fall and winter recuperating and making plans for the 2003 season. A prospective full-time ride in the NASCAR Busch Series failed to develop, but she intends to forge ahead.

"After what all I went through at Nashville, and the terrible tragedy at Lowe's, I feel like I can stand anything that's thrown at me from now on," she said. "It was a very traumatic year, but I think I came through it more determined than ever. The critics aren't going to run me off."

***

I never knew Wendell Scott, the only black driver to win an official NASCAR race, but Bob Harmon did. Harmon, late president of Nashville Speedway, used to promote races down in Alabama, and he insisted that the color of Scott's skin was never a problem.

"I was pretty close to Wendell," Harmon told me once. "He used to run a lot of my races, and he had dinner in my house. We spent quite a bit of time together, and I think he'd have told me if he had any trouble.

"I always got the impression that Wendell was liked and respected by the other drivers. He didn't cause any problems, just showed and ran his race and minded his own business. He was a good driver, but like a lot of guys back then, he couldn't afford good equipment. He was forced to run a lot of junk. But he always did the best with what he had. I thought Wendell Scott was a helluva nice guy."

Scott is the only black driver to be inducted into the Motorsports Hall of Fame. Willie T. Ribbs tried unsuccessfully to break into NASCAR, first in the late 1970s and later in 2001, and was convinced that his color was a barrier.

"NASCAR today is like baseball in the 1940s," Ribbs once told me. "Baseball finally decided it was going to have black players and made it happen. If NASCAR really wanted to have black drivers, it could make it happen."

NASCAR, in recent years, has worked to open doors to minorities in all levels of the sport, from driving to marketing. In concert with Dodge Motorsports, NASCAR started a diversity program to train and develop minority participants.

I am convinced that NASCAR is serious about increasing its minority presence for a number of reasons. It would codify stock car racing as a true "mainstream" sport. It would provide a marketing boom, attracting a huge, untapped minority following. But most of all, I believe NASCAR realizes that it is simply the right thing to do.

Ribbs got an opportunity to drive in the NASCAR Craftsman Truck Series in 2001, but had little success. Another black driver, Bill Lester, replaced him in the Bobby Hamilton Racing truck. Although Lester failed to win in 2002, he showed signs of promise. Lester, a well-spoken college graduate, said he has encountered nothing but encouragement since he had been in NASCAR.

"Everyone has been great to me," he said. "I haven't had a single negative experience."

"Bill Lester is a good racer and as far as I'm concerned that's all that matters," Hamilton said. "I don't care if a driver is black, white or green. All I care about is whether he can drive that damn race car."

Unfortunately, not everyone shares Hamilton's sentiments. Just as Renshaw and other women drivers have encountered blatant sexism, there are undeniable strains of racism in racing. A couple of years ago I wrote a column praising NASCAR for its efforts to bring more blacks into the sport, an effort that was long overdue. I received hate mail; not a lot, but what did arrive was telling:

"NASCAR racing is the last sport where I watch a white man compete," said one letter. "Blacks have taken over football, basketball and baseball. I don't want them to take over racing."

"If they want to race, let them race," said another. "But don't hand them a free ride. They should have to go out and earn a ride just like white drivers do. It seems to me they don't want an opportunity, they want a handout from NASCAR."

There is a flaw in that logic. Granted, NASCAR has never had an official policy banning blacks from participation, but remember this: stock car racing began on small, rural, Southern tracks, in areas where blacks often were not permitted to eat at a public restaurant or drink from a public water fountain. Can you imagine a black driver showing up on a Saturday night at some little country bullring inhabited by rednecks and rowdies who frequently were drinking?

That was hardly a "career option" for blacks of that era.

Yes, Wendell Scott did it and survived, although according to legend when he won his lone NASCAR race in 1963 at Jacksonville, Fla., Scott was not allowed to come to the stage and accept his trophy. The track promoter feared there would be trouble from the all-white crowd if a black man were to be presented a trophy from a white, skimpily attired beauty queen. Scott's trophy was sent to him later.

That is the legacy that today's aspiring black drivers struggle against. The playing field in racing has not always been level.

"I never wanted a handout," Ribbs told me a few years ago. "All I ever asked for was an opportunity. Even if I don't make it, maybe I can get the attention of some little black kid and inspire him to give it a shot. Maybe someday when that little black kid grows up he will make it in NASCAR.

"Maybe it's too late for me, but it's not too late for him."

To NASCAR's credit, it's trying.

LAP XX:

INK-STAINED WRETCHES

Next time you're in Daytona, check out the swath of grass adjacent to the La Quinta motel, located just off the I-95 exit that leads to Daytona International Speedway. Look carefully and you'll find a bronze plaque, commemorating the spot where the infamous Boar's Head Lounge once stood.

The marker was put there by Bill Brodrick, who used to be the racing PR rep for Union 76. Brodrick back then wore a thick mane of golden hair, swept back, and had a ruddy complexion.

Veteran race fans might remember Brodrick as the "Hat Man" who used to always be in Victory Circle, placing a variety of caps on the head of the winning driver. (Each driver had a variety of different sponsors, and each sponsor naturally wanted a photo of the victor wearing his particular cap.)

Brodrick's primary function was overseeing the Union 76 Race Stoppers—a bevy of stunning young women whose assignment was to gather around the winning driver after each race and smother him with smooches while the flashbulbs popped. This was back before the PC Police decreed that using scantily clad young women for photo props was a sexist ruse and got it banished from practice—causing the demise of a great NASCAR postrace tradition.

Did I mention that Brodrick got to escort the Union 76 girls around in a flashy convertible with the Union 76 Racing logo on its side? As if that wasn't already a gig from heaven, Bill also had a lavish expense account and was not averse to picking up obscenely large bar tabs.

In the eyes of us writers, Bill Brodrick was a great and noble American.

Many of the aforementioned bar tabs were compiled in the aforementioned Boar's Head lounge, the most popular media hangout during Daytona's February Speed Weeks. Most of the media was headquartered at the adjacent Howard Johnson's (now La Quinta) and the Boar's Head was, as my buddy Joe Caldwell once remarked, "within easy crawling distance."

Many of the drivers and team officials in town for the big race also congregated at the Boar's Head, throwing money around and attracting flocks of attractive, available ladies (pit lizards).

The Boar's Head had a jukebox and sometimes a live band. (Why do they always advertise a "live band?" Caldwell always wondered. Who'd come to see a dead band?)

The Boar's Head featured a well-worn parquet dance floor next to the horseshoe-shaped bar, over which drinks cascaded like Niagara Falls right up to last call at 2:00 a.m.

One night, upon hearing the waitress behind the bar yell "Last call!" one sports writer rose to his feet and shouted, "I'd like to call Aunt Flo in Topeka!"

The Boar's Head was invariably crowded, smoky, loud, wild, and raucous. It was there, late one evening, that the legend of Rainbow Willie was born. Willie, a well-known writer, was merrily ensconced at the bar when a friendly young black woman joined him. Extremely friendly, in a professional manner, if you get my drift. She told Willie that for a certain price she would show him exactly how friendly she could be.

Terms were discussed and agreed on, and Willie and his new best friend left the Boar's Head arm in arm and repaired to his room. That's where Willie was discovered the next morning by the maids, hog-tied to his bed. It gets worse. He was buck naked.

Worse yet. He was body-painted from head to foot in all the hues of the rainbow.

Still worse: the young black hooker was a transvestite. And a thief.

After shackling Willie to the bed and painting him, the transvestite Picasso took Willie's wallet and absconded.

The housemaids untied Willie and the poor guy—having, in the past few hours, already made enough errors in judgment to last a lifetime—made one more: instead of showering himself off, cutting his losses, and keeping quiet about the entire episode, Willie called the police.

He told them exactly what had happened and they filed a report.

The next morning the Daytona paper ran a small story about an out-of-town sports writer who had been robbed in his hotel room. None of the juicy details were included in the story, but someone who knew someone in the police department found out what had happened. The complete account, with all the details about the paintbrush-wielding, body-painting, bed-strapping-down transvestite hooker leaked out.

A couple of Willie's good friends decided a story like that should be shared with the world. They typed up a lurid, spare-no-details account, made copies, and distributed one at every seat in the Daytona press box.

Someone later remarked that it was the best-read story of the entire Speed Weeks. The colorful legend of Rainbow Willie was born, a reference to which is today emblazoned in bronze on a plaque on the spot where the Boar's Head once squatted.

In fairness to Willie, he was not the only sports writer to yield to temptation while traveling the lonely road. Long nights, neon lights, and expense-account drinks can be a lethal combination.

Along for the Ride 185

The late Atlanta humor columnist and author Lewis Grizzard, a devoted NASCAR fan, related this oft-told story in one of his books:

"A sports writer is propped up at the bar when he is approached by a sultry Lady of the Evening. They strike up a conversation. Conversation progresses into negotiation. She whispers that she'll do anything he wants for $50.

"Anything?" says the sports writer.

"Anything," she coos in his ear.

"OK then," he says, reaching for his wallet. "Here's $50. Go up to my room and write me a column."

***

A favorite pastime for sports writers on the road is sitting around swapping favorite newspaper headlines and bloopers.

A story about a golf pro offering free lessons for ladies was headlined: "Women Get Hot Tits." (Tips.)

From the world of basketball:

"...he raced to mid-court, where he took a desperate shit..."

My contribution is one that ran on the *Tennessean*'s outdoor page underneath a photo of a well-endowed young lady in a bikini perched atop a new boat. Bill Isom, the headline writer, wanted to pay tribute to both the young woman and the handsome craft—unaware that the boat would be cropped out of the picture. Next morning the paper carried a photo of the large-chested woman, and beneath, the caption: "A Pair of Beauties!"

You had to be careful when Dick Trickle was in the race.

"Dick Trickle brings out a caution!" "So-and-so was taken out by Dick Trickle."

Trickle, a veteran driver with an estimated 1,200 short-track victories to his credit, doesn't race much any more, prompting one commentator to sadly remark: "It's too bad that a lot of today's NASCAR fans don't know Dick."

Back to headlines, this may be the all-time classic:

A woman's golf tournament paired the top players from different courses around town to determine the best of the best. After the final round, a banner headline proudly proclaimed: "Marge Jones Wins Inter-Course Championship."

"Now there," drawled Jim McLaurin of the Columbia (S.C.) *State*, "is a headline that makes you want to read on."

***

As I explained earlier, I became a racing writer the same way I became an army infantryman—I was drafted. A lot of my fellow writers—"ink-stained wretches" as Tom Higgins of the *Charlotte Observer* used to call us—followed a similar career path to pit road.

Joe Caldwell, my best friend on the planet for over 30 years, wrote for *The Nashville Banner*, the afternoon paper and *The Nashville Tennessean*'s archrival. Caldwell was short and bald—we called him "Baldwell"—and he was an excellent writer, among the best in racing. Caldwell had been a stick-and-ball writer who had never covered racing until, like me, his editor assigned him to the beat.

Caldwell began covering NASCAR about two years before I did. Even though we competed fiercely for stories, we were best friends, as close as any brothers.

For three decades we traveled together, roomed together, wrote together, caroused together, laughed together and at times got in trouble together.

Once, stuck in postrace traffic in Talladega, Caldwell honked at a stalled car in front of us. A burly Alabama state trooper, crimson-faced and dripping sweat, stormed over and rapped on the window with his Billy club.

"What the hell you honkin' at?" he snarled.

"Uh, slow traffic?" Caldwell simpered

The cop made us pull out of line and sit on the curb for an hour.

During another trip to Talladega, Caldwell—always in a hurry—swerved in front of an ancient, rust-scabbed pickup truck as it wobbled along. Immediately it speeded up, and we found ourselves being chased by two obviously drunken rednecks. I noticed there was a gun rack in the back of their truck.

"Damn you, Caldwell," I sputtered as we fled our pursuers, "if they catch us you'd better hope they shoot me first, because if I'm still alive I'm going to help them beat the hell out of you!"

Joe outran the rednecks, but he couldn't outrun Coo Coo Marlin, the crusty old racer from Columbia.

We had attended a Speedway awards dinner one fine autumn evening, and afterwards Coo Coo and his wife Eula Faye suggested that we all meet at a nightclub on the outskirts of town for a nightcap. Coo Coo, it should be noted, was already well into his nightcapping. For some reason (premonition?) I declined the invitation, but Caldwell and his date accepted.

Caldwell pulled out of the parking lot and Coo Coo and Eula Faye followed them to the interstate entrance ramp.

"Coo Coo came roaring up behind me and suddenly I felt a thump on my rear bumper," Caldwell said. "He had hit me. I thought, 'What the hell—' then, wham! He hit me again. And again.

"I speeded up. Coo Coo speeded up. I went faster. He went faster. He bumped me again. By now I was going about 85 miles an hour and he was still bumping me. My date was whimpering and begging me to slow down. I decided this was crazy; I wasn't going to go any faster.

"I lifted off the gas, but the car didn't slow down. Coo Coo was pushing me down the interstate! We got up to about 90 and I knew that if I hit my brakes it would wreck us all.

"Finally, just as we got to our exit, Coo Coo backed off and I managed to swerve up the ramp.

"When we got to the nightclub a few minutes later my hands were still shaking and my date was almost hysterical. That damn-fool Coo Coo could have killed us. I climbed from the car just as he and Eula Faye pulled up beside us. Coo Coo was laughing his head off, and Eula Faye was cussing and pounding on him with her fists.

"That night I got a pretty good idea about what drivers who raced against Coo Coo Marlin went through. He was wild and crazy as hell, and he wasn't afraid to do anything."

Caldwell and I once played golf with Jimmy Spencer. A beer cart followed us around, and by the end of the round Spencer was driving up to his ball and swatting it with his club from the moving cart, a la polo. I wish I'd kept that scorecard.

Caldwell possessed a wicked sense of humor. In a media golf tournament at Talladega he and I were paired with Neil Bonnett and an area banker. It was a drizzly, blustery day and we all played terribly. Even Caldwell, normally an excellent golfer, turned into a total hacker.

Finally, mercifully, we trudged up to the 18th hole. Caldwell was up.

"It's your turn, last hole," the banker said to Caldwell over the howling wind.

"Who you calling an ass hole?" snapped Caldwell, whirling around. "You didn't play so damned well yourself!"

The startled banker turned crimson and began to sputter an apology. Bonnett, aware of what a prankster Caldwell was, roared with laugher.

***

Caldwell and I attended the annual Winston Media Party at Daytona's posh Pelican Bay Country Club one year where a striking young lady in an elegant evening gown was serving as hostess.

Her name was Brooke Sealey. Caldwell went over and asked her to dance. She accepted. He was enchanted. After the dance ended, I offered to hold Joe's jacket while he went and took a cold shower.

Brooke Sealey eventually became Mrs. Jeff Gordon. The marriage didn't last, unfortunately. Some of us were not surprised;

we always figured that Brooke had been spoiled by the magical evening when she danced with Caldwell. No other man could ever measure up.

Caldwell and I were in New York one winter for the NASCAR Winston Cup awards banquet when a mini-skirted young lady sidled up to him at the bar at the swanky Waldorf. She slipped Joe her phone number and told him to give her a call later. She said she would "show him the city."

When we got back to the room Caldwell, at the time a bachelor, decided to dial the number—just out of curiosity, of course.

I heard his end of the conversation:

"Hi, Trina, it's me, Joe."

Pause.

"Sure, that sounds like fun."

Pause.

"What? HOW MUCH?"

Caldwell carefully hung up the phone.

"I thought she wanted to go on a date," he said, "not sell me a car."

***

The Nashville Banner folded a few years ago. Like many evening newspapers it was a victim of a changing news market. Caldwell was in Daytona when his wife Cathy called with the news.

"The phone rang in my room early that morning," Joe recalled later, "and when I answered, the first thing Cathy said was, 'I hope the paper gave you a round-trip ticket.'"

Caldwell died a year later of a sudden heart attack. We had been to a downtown roast for MTSU football coach Boots Donnelly on a Friday night. Every major sports personality in Nashville was there, laughing, joking, and telling stories. Caldwell should have been in his element—fun, friends and frivolity—but he was uncharacteristically quiet all evening. He said he felt tired. I told him he was just getting old.

We left around midnight. Cathy called early the next morning in tears. Joe was dead.

We had spent over 30 years together, a great 30 years.

Caldwell's gone, and racing—and life itself—isn't as much fun any more.

***

A lot of the Old Gang has departed. Caldwell died. So did Chattanooga's Connor Gilbert and Virginia's Gerald Martin. Atlanta's George Cunningham died, and his replacement, Tom McCollister, covered the beat for several years before losing his life in a car crash.

Bud Burns, the World War II hero and gruff old editor who sent me to cover my first race, is dead. So are Bill Isom and F. M. Williams (of Eddie Gossage/telecopier fame). So are my old sports editors: Raymond Johnson, who hired me, and John Bibb, who assigned me to the racing beat over 30 years ago.

I don't know what became of Boog. Someone said he moved to New York. I didn't know they had a Tootsie's up there.

Birmingham's Clyde Bolton—maybe the best writer ever—retired from newspapering and is writing books. Knoxville's Bill Luther retired, as did Virginia's Frank Vehorn and Charlotte's Tom Higgins. (The irrepressible Higgins, upon spotting a pretty girl at the track, would boom, "Fire in the hole, boys!" Or, "Bird in the bush!" Or, simply, "Merciful God!")

Steve Waid became an editor for the influential racing tabloid, NASCAR Winston Cup Scene, and also has a TV gig. It's good to see a charter member of "Brothers of the Towel" succeed, even though Waid no longer wears cloth dinner napkins on his head. Franks roadhouse burned down. Boss Hogg discontinued his pool parties. Bob Latford retired, but still occasionally shows up at races.

That reminds me of a sports writer in Memphis who retired briefly, then returned to the paper, prompting a cynical fellow staffer to remark:

"The stupid SOB broke out of prison then broke back in!"

***

A racing writer once stumbled into his motel room after a long, hard night on the town.

Knowing that he had a full day at the track ahead of him, he fumbled for the phone, dialed the front desk, and told the clerk he wanted to leave a wakeup call.

"Certainly, sir," said the clerk. "And for what time?"

"Make it for six o'clock," said the writer.

"I'm sorry, sir, but I can't do that," said the clerk.

"Why'n hell not?" growled the writer.

"Because it's 6:15 now, sir," replied the clerk to the poor, ink-stained wretch.

Celebrate the Heroes of Stock Car Racing
in These Other Acclaimed Titles from Sports Publishing!

Sterling Marlin: The Silver Bullet
by Larry Woody
- 10 x 10 hardcover
- 128 pages
- 100 color photos throughout
- $39.95
- Includes cdracecard CD-ROM

Flat Out and Half Turned Over: Tales from Pit Road with Buddy Baker
by Buddy Baker and David Poole
- 5.5 x 8.25 hardcover
- 169 pages
- photos throughout
- $19.95

Jeff Gordon: Burning Up the Track
by the *Indianapolis Star and News*
- 10 x 10 hardcover • 100 pages
- color photos
- Includes 60-minute audio CD
- $39.95
- **2003 release!**

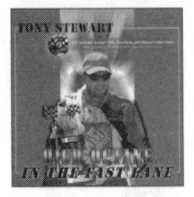

Tony Stewart: High Octane in the Fast Lane
by the Associated Press
- 10 x 10 hardcover
- 160 pages
- color photos
- Includes 60-minute audio CD
- $39.95
- **2003 release!**

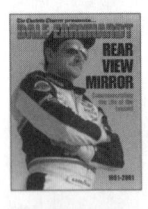

As They Head for the Checkers: Fantastic Finishes, Memorable Milestones and Heroes Remembered from the World of Racing
by Kathy Persinger and Mark Garrow (audio)
- 8.5 x 11 h/c • 160 pages • color & b/w photos • Includes audio CD • $39.95 • **2003 release!**

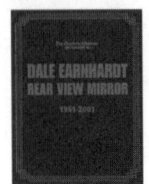

The History of America's Greatest Stock Car Tracks: From Daytona to the Brickyard
by Kathy Persinger
- Race track shaped hardcover
- 160 pages • color & b/w photos
- $29.95

Dale Earnhardt: The Pass in the Grass and Other Incredible Moments from Racing's Greatest Legend
by *The Charlotte Observer* and Mark Garrow (audio)
- 10.5 x 10.5 hardcover • 160 pages • color and b/w photos
- Includes audio CD • $39.95

StockcarToons 2: More Grins and Spins on the Winston Cup Circuit
by Mike Smith, cartoonist for the *Las Vegas Sun*
- 11 x 8.5 softcover • 160 pages
- cartoons throughout • $12.95
- **2003 release!**

StockcarToons: Grins and Spins on the Winston Cup Circuit
by Mike Smith, cartoonist for the *Las Vegas Sun*
- 11 x 8.5 softcover • 160 pages
- cartoons throughout • $12.95

Dale Earnhardt: Rear View Mirror
by *The Charlotte Observer*
- 8.5 x 11 hardcover and softcover
- 209 pages • 160+ color and b/w photos throughout
- $29.95 (hardcover)
- $22.95 (softcover)

Dale Earnhardt: Rear View Mirror (leatherbound edition)
by *The Charlotte Observer*
- 8 1/2 x 11 leatherbound • 209 pages
- 160+ color and b/w photos
- $49.95
- **Limited to 1,000 copies!**

Richard Petty: The Cars of the King
by Tim Bongard and Bill Coulter
- 8.5 x 11 hardcover and softcover
- 259 pages
- 500+ color and b/w photos
- $34.95 (hardcover)
- $24.95 (softcover)
- $99.95 (leatherbound)
- **Leatherbound Edition signed by Richard Petty!**

To order at any time, please call toll-free **877-424-BOOK (2665)**.
For fast service and quick delivery, order on-line at **www.SportsPublishingLLC.com**.